FAT BOY AND THE CHAMPAGNE SALESMAN

FAT BOY AND THE CHAMPAGNE SALESMAN

Göring, Ribbentrop, and the Nazi Invasion of Poland

Rush Loving Jr.

INDIANA UNIVERSITY PRESS

This book is a publication of

Indiana University Press
Office of Scholarly Publishing
Herman B Wells Library 350
1320 East 10th Street
Bloomington, Indiana 47405 USA

iupress.org

Manufactured in the United States of America
First printing 2022

Cataloging information is available from the Library of Congress.

ISBN 978-0-253-06194-2 (hdbk.)
ISBN 978-0-253-06195-9 (pbk.)
ISBN 978-0-253-06196-6 (web PDF)

*To my two best friends, my sister Anne Loving Fenley
and my wife Jane Gregory Loving.*

CONTENTS

PREFACE

MOST PEOPLE KNOW THAT WORLD WAR II BEGAN because Hitler demanded the return of the Polish Corridor, a strip of German land that had been given to Poland at the end of World War I. Few are aware of the struggle that went on inside Hitler's Reich Chancellery that led to the invasion of Poland. It was a dramatic battle between Hitler's two top lieutenants, Hermann Göring and Joachim von Ribbentrop.

Fifty years ago, the cause of the war intrigued me, but when I began research for a book on the subject, I found that new information was coming to light almost every month. So I bided my time and collected source material as it emerged into public view.

I started with sources such as *Documents of German Foreign Policy, The British War Blue Book, The French Yellow Book,* and the diary of Italian foreign minister Galeazzo Ciano. But in the 1960s, a rich stream of additional material began to surface, and the flow continued into the twenty-first century. This material included the memoirs and diary of Albert Speer and the memoirs of generals Wilhelm Keitel and Franz Halder, as well as memoirs on life with Adolf Hitler. Finally, through Baltimore's Enoch Pratt Free Library, I borrowed a copy of the memoir of Göring's secret emissary to the British government, a Swedish businessman named Birger Dahlerus, who plays a major role in this book.

Originally, I pieced together a story of diplomats and their governments maneuvering to get what they wanted while hopefully avoiding a war. It was a fascinating yarn. But the more sources I unearthed, the more I began to focus on an even more compelling—and dramatic—side story. Göring and Ribbentrop, I discovered, pulled Hitler in different directions, as Göring desperately tried to avoid a war with Britain, and Ribbentrop, insisting the British would back down, urged Hitler to push them all the way. It is a sensational yarn—one that includes scenes of Hitler ordering his generals to pull back their troops even as they marched toward the Polish border.

Thus, *Fat Boy and the Champagne Salesman.*

FAT BOY AND THE CHAMPAGNE SALESMAN

INTRODUCTION

Adolf Hitler's Bequest

WHEN AMERICANS TRAVEL TO THE BATTLEFIELD AT NORMANDY'S Pointe du Hoc, invariably they visit the nearby cemetery where US soldiers are buried. There lie ten thousand men who gave their lives for the cause of freedom.

The graveyard most people do not see is nine miles east, at La Cambe, one of six where the German dead rest. It is even more moving than the American burial ground. There lie more than twenty-one thousand men— many who, at the time of their deaths, were in their midteens, others as old as seventy. Most of them had been conscripted into a war that none had ever wanted, for a regime many did not believe in.

They were there because Reichsmarschall Hermann Göring, known by some of the other generals as Fat Boy, had been losing a secret battle with a onetime champagne salesman named Joachim von Ribbentrop, who had become Germany's foreign minister.

As a result, in August 1939, Adolf Hitler made one of the most tragic decisions in history.

1

KAISER WILHELM'S LEGACY

WORLD WAR II PROBABLY NEVER WOULD HAVE OCCURRED had it not been for Kaiser Wilhelm II. The Nazi Party would not have taken over Germany, and the Communists would not have seized control of the Russian Empire. Life in the last three-quarters of the twentieth century would have been radically different. In fact, there never would have been cause to write this book.

Wilhelm had made a mutual-assistance pact with Franz Josef, emperor of the Austro-Hungarian Empire, in 1914. The empire had stretched across southern Europe, from the Italian and Swiss borders on the west to Romania and the Russian Empire in the east. It extended halfway down the eastern coast of the Adriatic Sea.

Among those lands to Austria's south lay the principalities of Bosnia and Herzegovina, which had been annexed by Austria-Hungary in 1908. Serbs, who wanted to create a Balkan nation from those two provinces, Serbia, and other states in the region, had been outraged. In June 1914, the heir to the Austrian throne, Archduke Franz Ferdinand, and his wife were visiting Bosnia's principal city, Sarajevo, when a group of Serbs assassinated them. Austria soon went to war against Serbia, and because of Wilhelm's mutual-assistance pact with Franz Josef, Germany was forced to support the Austrians. Great Britain, France, Italy, and Russia soon stood up against the two nations, igniting World War I.

The war was brutal. Modern weapons were used against men fighting with nineteenth-century tactics, and the result was a merciless slaughter on both sides. Soldiers were sent charging across battlefields as they had for centuries only to be mowed down by modern machine guns. They fought from trenches deep enough for men to move about without being shot. But they still could be killed by poison gas or modern artillery shells that created mammoth gaps in the line or by airplanes that could fly over and strafe everyone below. Much of that generation of Europe's men died. France and Germany each lost 16 percent of their fighting men. Britain lost 10 percent.

The civilians of Germany suffered as well. The British set up a naval blockade that cut Germany's food supply, and the shortage was made worse because the military took much of the farmers' output. Hundreds of thousands of Germans and Austrians starved and many died.

Even though they were fighting Germany, Russians starved as well, inciting food riots that brought on the Russian Revolution. The war that Wilhelm helped to set off cost his cousin Nicholas II his throne and later his life. It also planted the seeds for Communism, which has infected the world up to the present day.

Eventually, Germany surrendered and the people soon revolted, forcing Wilhelm to flee to neutral Holland, where he spent the remainder of his life.

When the victors met at France's Palace of Versailles to put together a peace treaty, they punished Germany harshly. On its western border, Germany was required to return the provinces of Alsace and Lorraine, which it had seized from France after the Franco-Prussian War in 1871. In addition, Germany's Rhineland was turned into a demilitarized zone where German troops were forbidden to venture.

In the east, Germany's loss was much dearer. More than a century before, Germany and Russia had divided the ancient state of Poland between themselves, allowing Austria one of Poland's duchies. The Treaty of Versailles re-created Poland, taking back the lands that the three nations held. Poland received large portions of eastern Germany, including part of Prussia, the state where the German Empire had been born. The treaty gave Poland access to the Baltic Sea through a narrow corridor of Prussian land that separated Germany from the remainder of Prussia. The strip included the German port of Danzig, which was made a free city, meaning it belonged to no nation.

But that was not all. The most injurious of the punishments were economic. Before the war, Germany and Britain had been Europe's two most affluent economic powers. That ended. Germany had been the world's third-largest colonial empire, with lands in Africa and the Pacific, some of which were abundant with natural resources. That ended too. The treaty stripped all those colonies away, removing a treasured source of income. In a move that further crippled Germany's economy, France was given the Saar's coalfields for fifteen years, and Germany's agriculture was impaired as well because the grants to Poland had included some of Germany's most fertile farmlands.

Those takings left the economy in tatters. Moreover, the treaty required that Germany pay the victors 132 billion gold marks in reparations to help compensate them for the cost of the war, which had drained their treasuries. Britain, France, and Belgium were in recession, and the French and Belgians were strained even more than the British because much of their lands had been the battlefield and they were having to rebuild.

The reparations were supposed to help compensate Britain and France, but that cost and the loss of colonies and fertile farmland devastated Germany yet more. Inflation soon struck, causing the cost of living to soar by more than sixteen times in only six months. Some of the payments were to be made in shipments of coal, timber, and other commodities, and when Germany defaulted on its shipments, France and Belgium occupied the Ruhr, home of Germany's steel industry.

All this created what would become a long-standing resentment among the Germans—and a growing demand that those lost lands be reclaimed and the Treaty of Versailles be negated. It all was a recipe for insurrection, tyranny, and war.[1]

2

THE ELOQUENT ARTIST

The guards wore black uniforms with silver insignia and polished black helmets. Some sat in machine-gun emplacements that surrounded the Berghof. Others stood alert, their rifles slung over their shoulders. They all were the elite, and they well knew it, members of the Leibstandarte, the führer's bodyguard of specially selected members of the Schutzstaffel, the dreaded SS, the Nazi Party's military arm.

The sun was rising slowly over the Alps. The Berghof sat on the mountainside in the settlement of Obersalzberg, eleven miles up the mountain from the town of Berchtesgaden in the southeast corner of Bavaria. The guards on the north side of the Berghof could see Austria, twenty miles away. It was August, and the day would be warm and free of the fog and drizzle that often hung over the mountains.

The Berghof symbolized Hitler's rise from a poor man to the rank of der führer, or leader, of all of Germany. He had organized the National Socialist, or Nazi, Party, which attracted many rich contributors. They saw the Nazis as their bulwark against the Communists, who would have stripped them of their wealth. So the party's treasury was flush, and Hitler and other Nazi leaders used it to live in splendor. It was a dramatic move up for a wretched street artist who had peddled nondescript little paintings to tourists. Now he was waited on by numerous servants, including a chauffeur, a valet, and a chef from one of Berlin's better restaurants. His habits could be a mixture of modesty and self-indulgence. He shaved himself each morning, but he insisted on having his valet supply him with a different blade for each side of his face.[1]

Adolf Hitler was a late sleeper, and the day was well on and growing warmer when his valet, Karl Wilhelm Krause, pushed a button outside his bedroom door that rang a bell attached to the headboard, signaling it was time to wake up.[2] As Hitler put on his jacket, he could see the firs standing on the opposite mountainside, warming in the Alpine sunlight. To Hitler, this was what made the Berghof home: the freedom, the space, and the peaceful beauty of a summer's day. The house had once been a modest Bavarian chalet, but using Nazi Party money and royalties from his book, *Mein Kampf*, the führer had turned it into the most impressive mansion in Germany.

* * *

Born in 1889 and raised in the Austrian city of Linz on the Danube, Adolf Hitler was a thin, weak child. His father, a customs officer, who was overbearing and sometimes brutal with him, had tried to get the rebellious boy to join the civil service, where he would have had to submit to authority, a fate young Hitler considered unthinkable. He scorned what he called such "bread and butter" jobs[3] and was intent on becoming a great painter.

Because of the venality he and his party represented, Hitler has been depicted as a madman. Actually, he is believed to have been bipolar.[4] As a boy, he was often moody and avoided friendships, and, like many manic-depressive people, in mere seconds he could swing unexpectedly from being mellow to possessing a raging anger that was, as his foreign minister said, "uncontrollable."[5] As a friend described him as a teenager, "Adolf was exceedingly violent and highly strung." A few meaningless words could set him off.[6]

Sometime in his youth, Hitler developed a hatred of Jews. Antisemitism was strong in Austria and Germany and, during economic downturns, German workers often became anticapitalists and blamed their plights on the Jews. But Hitler's hatred was far more intense than that of most. Although some psychologists have theorized about it, there is no sure way of knowing why.

During his teenage years, Hitler discovered he had a talent for speechmaking. If someone mentioned a subject that triggered him, Hitler would launch into a long, well-articulated speech about it.[7] Like his two chief wartime opponents, Franklin Roosevelt and Winston Churchill, Hitler could capture millions of listeners with his eloquence. While the words of Roosevelt and Churchill appealed more to the intellect, Hitler knew how to rouse people who were unhappy with the status quo. More ominously, his speeches could rouse a mob to rebellion and insurrection.

Hitler's deep voice was well suited to the task. At times, it was melodious, but when he wanted to stir his crowd into a frenzy, it turned into a shriek. He protected that voice and nurtured it by refraining from smoking. As a soldier in World War I, Hitler had smoked and drunk beer, but after the war, as he became interested in politics and speechmaking, he quit both.[8] His speeches ignited a loyalty in his German followers so blind and unswerving that those people enabled him to create an ironclad tyranny.

His personality was like that of many other leaders. Hitler's upbringing had been modest, and like some other successful politicians, he had a mammoth ego and an insatiable desire for power to compensate for his insecurity. Coupled with that, he was driven, a man obsessed with achieving his goals.[9] He could be manipulative and duplicitous or loose with the truth. Hitler also was impetuous and refused to listen to people who disagreed with him. And his subordinates were to give him their unswerving loyalty.

Even friends did not dare criticize or stand up to him. One of his oldest associates, Dr. Ernst "Putzi" Hanfstaengl, was the son of an old royalist family that had supported Otto von Bismarck when Kaiser Wilhelm II had dismissed his famous chancellor. Hanfstaengl met Hitler when the Nazi Party was a tiny, impoverished movement. When he came to power, Hitler made Hanfstaengl his liaison officer with the foreign press. They were so close that Hanfstaengl felt free to stand up to the führer on occasion, causing him to lose favor. Hitler eventually banned him from his presence, and in 1937, he had his underlings plot Hanfstaengl's execution. When Hanfstaengl discovered the death plot, he fled to Switzerland and then to London.[10]

Hitler read numerous biographies of world leaders, but as an assessment by the American intelligence service revealed, "his interest was confined to the demagogic, propagandistic and militaristic side."[11] Hitler also was a staunch believer in the use of force. "He considered toughness the supreme virtue of a man and interpreted emotion as weakness," said Otto Dietrich, Hitler's press secretary. Moreover, Dietrich held that Hitler's belief in the use of force blinded him to the sense of morality that guided the foreign policies of democratic nations.[12]

Unlike most other politicians, Hitler had no experience managing any organization. In fact, he had none of the self-discipline and the tolerance of routine that was required of good administrators. Yet he could pretend he tolerated routine. Normally, Hitler stayed up late and slept late. But when Field Marshal Paul von Hindenburg, Germany's president, was still active, Hitler was in his office next door to Hindenburg's palace every morning at ten o'clock. When Hindenburg lay dying at his estate in East Prussia, Hitler slept much later.[13]

Hitler's only career had been speechmaking, taking advantage of the country's hard times and stirring up listeners who were disenchanted, winning their support and creating a cult that imprisoned, tortured, and slaughtered its opponents.

Hitler understood drama, an instinct that led him to build the massive rally ground in Nuremberg, where every year he would harangue his followers, most of them lined up outfitted in the brown uniform of the Nazi Party.

For those close enough to have a conversation with him, Hitler's cold blue eyes bore into them and captivated them. Those eyes were so expressive they seemed to convey his moods and very thoughts.[14]

Adding to that, as he became active in the fledgling Nazi Party, Hitler created a physical image that was unforgettable. He shaved off a scraggly goatee and grew a strange square black mustache.[15] He also began combing his hair down across his left forehead and parting it so that a pointed lock hung over his eye. That, the mustache, and his blue eyes made Hitler distinct.

He even looked at his name with an eye to his future image. Hitler's father, Alois, had been illegitimate and had taken his mother's name, Schicklgruber. Later, a relative named Hiedler bequeathed a small legacy to Alois on condition that he adopt his name. Alois changed it accordingly, but with the spelling of *Hitler*, which sounded the same as *Hiedler*. Adolf later told a friend it was the best thing "the old man" had ever done, because the two other names were common but people would remember "Hitler."[16]

When he was eighteen, his mother died, and Hitler left Linz for Vienna, where he painted small pictures of the city and sold them on street corners. When World War I erupted, Hitler joined the Bavarian wing of the German army, rising to what some of his Prussian-born generals later disdained as the lowly rank of corporal.

After the Treaty of Versailles was imposed on them, the German people were resentful and restless. Before the war, Germany had been one of the world's greatest industrial powers, excelled only by the United States and Great Britain.

While Britain had been swept into the Industrial Revolution during the first half of the nineteenth century, Germany did not industrialize until decades later. In the last half of the nineteenth century, when Bismarck was Germany's chancellor, Germany had been transformed virtually overnight from an agricultural nation into an industrial powerhouse.

When Bismarck had begun his transformation, two-thirds of the German people had lived in the countryside, but by the outbreak of World War I, one-third of them had moved to the cities to work in the factories. In the process, Germany had created chemical giants like BASF and one of the world's leading pharmaceutical companies, Bayer. As electric power had begun to light the cities, Germany had become a leader in electrical parts and machines. Most important, Germany had replaced Britain as Europe's largest steelmaker, producing twice what the English were turning out. In Essen, the Krupp works had developed a metal that could be cast into the world's finest cannons, making Germany Europe's premier munitions maker.

Britain had watched with growing concern as Germany had become its chief economic rival. So it was natural for the British to be worried about the Germans—and for the Germans to feel threatened by the British. When England, France, and Russia formed an alliance at the turn of the century, the Germans believed they were being encircled.

During the last thirty years of the nineteenth century, Germany also had joined the race for colonies and had become the world's third-largest colonial empire, surpassed only by France and, of course, Britain, whose holdings spanned the globe. German colonies were scattered from New Guinea and the islands of the South Pacific to Africa, where German settlers were sending home boatloads of bananas, coffee, and cotton. Most important, the colonies' mines had rich lodes of copper, diamonds, and gold.

* * *

Reeling from the Treaty of Versailles, Germany was impoverished. Jobs were difficult to find, and people were scrambling to feed their families. Adding to the Germans' discontent, Russia's Communist government had caused many small business owners, many of them Jews, to leave, and they had flooded into Germany, often competing with the Germans for jobs.

Having an influx of immigrants invade the job market was bad enough, but for centuries, the Germans had viewed the Jews as inferior, confining them to ghettos. Additionally, the Communists were agitating in the streets for control of the German government. It all paved the way for opportunistic politicians, and Adolf Hitler took advantage of it.

After his discharge from the army, Hitler had settled in the southern state of Bavaria, a mountainous place occupied by conservative farmers and mountain people. These were people ripe for Hitler's message that the sins of Versailles must be overturned, the Communists put down, and the Jews kept out of German business and society. He joined a movement called the National Socialist German Workers' Party, or the Nazis, and soon was their speechmaker, demanding that the diktat of Versailles be rectified and attacking Communists and Jews.

The people took to his message. All of them were won over by Hitler's eloquence and a distinctive voice that Kurt Krueger, his doctor, described as "weird and compelling, like a Delphic oracle." Hitler had an uncanny feel for how his audience was reacting to his words, said Krueger, and he knew precisely what words to use next.[17] Soon, Hitler was attracting hundreds, then thousands, of followers, and he took over as the party's leader. In 1922, he led a small group of followers through the streets of Munich, attempting to overturn the Bavarian government in what came to be called the Beer Hall Putsch. They were stopped, and some of Hitler's cohorts were killed or wounded. Unscathed, Hitler stood trial and was sent to Landsberg Prison, where he was given lush quarters equal to an apartment, far above the dungeons in which he later confined his opponents. While in prison, Hitler spent his time writing *Mein Kampf,* a political testament that soon became a best seller and the Nazis' bible.

Before long, the Nazis began winning seats in the German parliament, or Reichstag, and in 1933, they won control, making Hitler Germany's chancellor. A year later, when Field Marshal von Hindenburg died and left the presidency vacant, Hitler seized that post as well, declaring himself the nation's führer, or supreme leader.

Simultaneously, the Nazis began suppressing dissent. Anyone who differed with Hitler or his policies was thrown into a concentration camp, an invention that would taint Germany for decades to come. Jews were persecuted as well. Those who worked for the government or universities soon lost their jobs, and people began to boycott Jewish businesses.

Hitler also began undoing the Treaty of Versailles. He viewed Great Britain, or England as it was known in Europe, as the greatest potential obstacle to his plans. Hitler's goal was to regain all the power and prestige that the treaty had swept away. He wanted those colonies returned, and more important, he wanted to recover the parts of Germany itself that Versailles had taken.

In 1935, Hitler saw an opportunity when Italy's Fascist dictator, Benito Mussolini, invaded Ethiopia. The British navy could have stopped him because the Italian fleet was supplying the invasion through the Suez Canal, which England controlled. Although the civilized world was shocked by the invasion, the British allowed the ships to keep passing in and out unchallenged. Seeing that, Hitler concluded that England feared war and could be bullied.[18]

His first move was to rebuild the armed forces, which was a blatant violation of the Treaty of Versailles. The English did nothing. He also announced that he was creating a new empire, the third in the history of Germany and Prussia. He called it the Third Reich, declaring it would last a thousand years.

Then, soon after Mussolini's invasion of Ethiopia, Hitler marched his army into the demilitarized Rhineland. Again, there was little objection from England.

Hitler went on to his next step. The treaty had forbidden Germany from uniting with Austria, and in March 1938, Hitler invited the country's chancellor, Kurt Schuschnigg, to his mountain retreat, where he forced him to consent to Germany's takeover of Austria.[19] With great fanfare, German troops marched in, and Hitler himself rode into Vienna to cement the union. Europe was shocked, but neither Britain nor France tried to stand in Hitler's way.[20]

So far, Hitler's instincts were proving right: most British people wanted no part of another war. They had lost a generation of young men in World War I, roughly seven hundred thousand of them, and they had no desire to sacrifice more lives merely to preserve the Treaty of Versailles. Nevertheless, many of the common people were appalled at the Nazis' brutality, especially their suppression of dissent and their treatment of the Jews. The Conservative government's position was guided largely by Britain's aristocracy, which feared the growth of socialism and, most notably, the spread of Communism. Many even were sympathetic to the Nazis because they saw Germany as Europe's bulwark against Communist Russia. Yet there were voices in the Conservative Party calling for its leaders to stand up to Hitler.

Their opposition grew louder during the summer of 1938, when Hitler went further and demanded that parts of Czechoslovakia occupied by people of German background be given to Germany. The Treaty of Versailles had created the Czech Republic out of Austria and Hungary. The Sudetenland, which lay along Czechoslovakia's border with Germany, had belonged to Austria and was predominately German. More important, the Sudetenland contained the famous Škoda Works, one of the world's most respected munitions makers.

Hitler told his generals that the reason for his demand was purely defensive.[21] Prague, the Czech capital, was only about two hundred miles from Berlin, half the distance between Hitler's Berghof and Berlin. If Russia wanted to invade Germany, Czechoslovakia would be an ideal launchpad, and if Germany were to take on France or Britain, Czechoslovakia would make an ideal air base for their bombers.[22]

To agree to Hitler's demand would have meant giving him much or all of the Sudetenland, which comprised the northern one-third of Czechoslovakia. The Czechs had a mutual-assistance treaty with the French, who had a similar pact with the British. Thus, if one went to war, the other two were pledged to join in. The British government responded to the German demand by supporting France, which had a defensive alliance with the Czechs.

British prime minister Neville Chamberlain took over the negotiations. Chamberlain was a tall, thin, nondescript man whose most notable features were a large mustache and a set of bushy eyebrows. He came from a family of politicians and had spent his own political career dealing mostly with domestic issues. Chamberlain knew little of foreign affairs and was an idealist who thought leaders like Hitler were gentlemen like all his friends.

Chamberlain met with Hitler on September 15 at the führer's Alpine home, where they sat down in the Berghof's great hall and Chamberlain gave in to Hitler's demand. He would return to London to get the approval of his cabinet, Chamberlain said.

A week later, Chamberlain returned to Germany for a second meeting, at a hotel on the Rhine in the town of Bad Godesberg. He had the acquiescence of the Czechs and the backing of the French, as well as his cabinet, and thought he was about to cement a deal to keep the peace. But Hitler surprised him by upping his demand. He also wanted parts of Czechoslovakia populated largely by Poles and Hungarians to be handed over to those two nations. And he gave Chamberlain an ultimatum: it all needed to be done by October 1, or he would seize what he wanted. Suddenly, Europe was panicked, overcome by fear of another war. The crisis resulted in a conference in Munich among Chamberlain, France's prime minister Édouard Daladier, and Hitler. Also there was Hitler's friend Benito Mussolini, who offered to broker the dispute. The Czechs were not invited.

They all gathered on September 29 in the Führerbau, a building that housed Hitler's Munich office. The session went on until the early hours of the following morning. Before attending the meeting, Chamberlain had given the world his own view of the Czechs, describing the crisis in a British

Fig. 2.1. The infamous meeting at Munich, at which the Sudetenland was taken from Czechoslovakia. The principals were (*from left*) Britain's Neville Chamberlain; Édouard Daladier of France; Adolf Hitler; Italy's dictator, Benito Mussolini; and Galeazzo Ciano, foreign minister of Italy and Mussolini's son-in-law.

radio broadcast as "a quarrel in a far away country between people of whom we know nothing." In that spirit, Chamberlain and Daladier gave Hitler the Sudeten and allowed the Poles and Hungarians to have the lands they wanted. Czechoslovakia was left a shadow of itself. For his part, Hitler promised that this would be his last territorial claim.

Before leaving for England, Chamberlain got Hitler to sign a paper saying Germany and Great Britain would never go to war again, and he arrived in England waving the document and declaring, "It means peace in our time." But as Winston Churchill retorted before the House of Commons, "We have sustained a total and unmitigated defeat." He added in the most somber of tones, "All is over. Silent, mournful, abandoned, broken, Czechoslovakia recedes into darkness."[23]

3

THE CHAMPAGNE SALESMAN

ADOLF HITLER WAS NAIVE ABOUT THE WORLD OUTSIDE Austria and Germany. It was the ignorance of an Austrian country boy, and as was the case with Neville Chamberlain, it was a dangerous attribute for a head of state. Except for fighting in France and Belgium and making two trips to Italy for meetings with Benito Mussolini, Hitler had never ventured outside Austria and Germany. He had little understanding of diplomacy and thought his foreign office professionals stuffy, out-of-touch aristocrats.

Accordingly, Hitler came under the influence of one of his followers, Joachim von Ribbentrop, who had toadied up to the führer and proclaimed himself an expert on the British and on foreign affairs in general. Ribbentrop had spent his youth in England and then Canada, where he had lived among German workers in British Columbia and the French in Quebec. At one point, he had gone to New York to work in a bank for a year.[1]

When World War I broke out, Ribbentrop had returned to Germany to serve in the army, where his father had been a career officer.[2] After the war, he became a champagne salesman and married into the family that produced Henkell, one of Europe's most prestigious sparkling wines. By law, the French had exclusive use of the term *champagne*, but the Germans called Henkell by that name anyway, and Ribbentrop's marriage put him in a position to provide Germany with one of the world's true champagnes, Pommery.

Ribbentrop's bride, Annelies Henkell, was a domineering woman who took charge of Joachim. She harbored an unrelenting hatred of the English, and despite the fact Ribbentrop had lived with an upper-class London family and made friends while in England, she soon instilled in him a similar dislike.

With help from his father-in-law, Ribbentrop set up an import-export business that specialized in champagnes and whiskeys. People considered him a good businessman—even inventive, on occasion—and the firm flourished.

Without question, Ribbentrop was a social climber and an opportunist, and sources suggest his wife had pushed him in that direction. Those who had met him before his marriage found a few years later that Ribbentrop had become arrogant and snobbish.[3] Although Ribbentrop's IQ was in fact high, his self-importance gave people the impression it was otherwise. As Frau Henkell put it, "It is odd that my dumbest son-in-law should have gone the farthest."[4]

Probably pushed by Annelies, Ribbentrop bought the title of *von* when he was thirty-two. A woman named Gertrud von Ribbentrop, the daughter of an army officer who had received the title for his services to the state, legally adopted Joachim, though the two were unrelated. She did so to preserve the family name—and because she was destitute. In return for the adoption, Ribbentrop agreed to pay her 450 Deutsche marks every month for fifteen years. Later, he tried to welch on his commitment and stop the payments, and she had to take him to court.[5]

As the Nazis gained prominence, Ribbentrop's wife became a convert, and apparently through her, he came to know some of the Nazi leaders. He finally joined the party in 1932, when it was apparent Hitler might become chancellor. The next year, Hitler and Franz von Papen, who had been chancellor, negotiated a deal that won Hitler that position, and when they needed a house for their secret meetings, Ribbentrop let them use his villa in the Berlin suburbs.[6]

Citing his time in England and North America during his youth and the many business contacts he maintained in France and Britain (he brought in more French Pommery and Scotland's Johnnie Walker, among other products), Ribbentrop soon convinced Hitler that he was a foreign affairs expert.[7] While the claim impressed Hitler, Ribbentrop really won over Hitler because he was a yes-man and knew how to massage Hitler's vanity.[8] The Ribbentrops even named their second son Adolf, winning the führer's favor all the more. Unfortunately, Hitler did not realize that this obsequious man could manipulate his boss, an ability that could prove fatal to the führer and to Germany.

The Treaty of Versailles limited Germany's navy to only a tiny fleet of aging ships. Accordingly, Hitler ordered Ribbentrop to go to London and negotiate a naval treaty with Great Britain. The Champagne Salesman dictated the terms of the treaty to the British, announcing that if they did not meet his demands, Germany would simply build whatever size navy it wanted. The English reluctantly agreed, giving Germany the right to build a fleet more than one-third the size of the British navy, the world's largest assembly of fighting ships.

Given that success, the next year, despite the objections of many leading Nazis, Hitler made Ribbentrop ambassador to England. Once in London, the Champagne Salesman cultivated friends among the pro-Nazi faction of the English upper class, thereby strengthening his belief that the British would never fight.

His arrogance, pomposity, and raging ineptitude soon made him a joke among many of the British. As he backed away and bowed after his presentation to the newly crowned king George VI, Ribbentrop threw up his arm in a Hitler salute.[9] The king might have been amused, but many Britons were not, and the incident inspired one of the country's leading cartoonists to make fun of Ribbentrop. Earlier, while Ribbentrop was attending an Anglican church service, the organist had begun playing the prelude to the hymn "Joyful! Joyful!"—the same tune as the German national anthem—and Ribbentrop had jumped to his feet, stretching out his arm in the Hitler salute, causing his embarrassed hostess to frantically pull him down.[10]

Although his duties were supposed to be in London, Ribbentrop spent much of his time in Berlin to be close to the führer, which annoyed the German foreign office. Modern critics would say he was there "sucking up," and the British soon dubbed him "Germany's part-time ambassador."[11]

Adolf Hitler was practically obsessed with the idea that Germany and England could be friends. He admired the English, believing that through their Anglo-Saxon lineage and the royal family's Teutonic bloodline, they were kin to the Germans. He ordered Ribbentrop to lure the British into signing a defense pact with Germany that would free his hand in eastern Europe. It was to be the Champagne Salesman's most important assignment. But the British were not interested, and Ribbentrop's failure to get his treaty likely further stoked Ribbentrop's hatred of the English.

One day, when Winston Churchill visited the German embassy to discuss a newspaper article he had written in which he mentioned the ambassador, Ribbentrop tried to gain his support for the Nazis' ambitions in eastern Europe. Churchill replied that he was certain the government would never agree to such an idea. Great Britain would never give Germany a free hand.

"In that case, war is inevitable," said Ribbentrop. "There is no way out. The führer is resolved."

"When you talk of war which, no doubt, would be a general war, you must not underrate England," Churchill warned. "Do not underrate England. She is very clever. If you plunge us all into another Great War, she will bring the whole world against you like last time."[12]

Ribbentrop's bumptious performance in London might have elicited the laughter or annoyance of the English, but not of Adolf Hitler. In 1938, the führer called Ribbentrop home to become Germany's foreign minister, much to the relief of many Englishmen, but to the concern of others and to the disgust of Nazi leaders such as Hermann Göring and Germany's propaganda minister, Joseph Goebbels.[13] "Ribbentrop was a boundless egotist, a wine salesman who was successful in business but had neither the background nor the tact for diplomacy," Göring later said.[14]

4

FAT BOY'S SWEDISH FRIEND

Encouraged by Germany's easy victory at Munich, Ribbentrop persuaded Hitler that this achievement had been so simple he should keep pushing the British. They still feared war, he assured the führer, and they would bend again to his demands.[1]

Hitler did not take the Munich Agreement very seriously. After Chamberlain had persuaded Hitler to sign the paper pledging they would never go to war again, Ribbentrop complained to the führer, and Hitler had calmed him, saying, "That scrap of paper is of no significance whatsoever."[2]

Next to reclaiming lands Germany had lost in Europe, the biggest issue Hitler needed to resolve with the British was the return of Germany's colonies. In particular, he wanted lands such as Tanganyika (now Tanzania) that produced gold and diamonds, as well as the colonies that had supplied boatloads of fruit and cotton.[3] In Hitler's view, the colonies would not only restore to the German people the prestige of owning an empire but also help Germany reign again as an economic power. Invariably, that would lead to a confrontation.

Hitler planned to raise the colonial question several years later, when Germany's military force would be stronger. Meanwhile, he would protect his eastern flank and retrieve the land Germany had lost to Poland.

Rather than viewing the English as an obstacle, Hitler had admired the way the British had built and kept their empire. Repeatedly, he'd told his friends how he always hoped for peace and friendship with the British. But now he began amending his position. Fired by the weak way they had confronted Mussolini over his invasion of Ethiopia, and his own triumph at Munich, Hitler began to feel he could walk over the English with ease.[4]

In that spirit, Hitler considered what he would demand next. Like most Germans, the führer was convinced the English had used their diktat at

Versailles to deliberately strip Germany of its rank as their greatest competitor. He believed, therefore, that he must always protect his back in the east while dealing with this adversary to the west. Germany's great threat in the east was the Soviet Union. The Russians and their Communist missionaries were Germany's eternal enemies.

They also were a threat to the Reich's eastern neighbor Poland, whose people had cause to fear the Russians. The Poles were adamant capitalists and, like the English and the Germans, felt threated by Communism. Moreover, the Soviet Union had been Poland's enemy, taking its lands whenever the opportunity arose. More recently, when Poland had seized part of Czechoslovakia during the Sudetenland crisis, relations with Russia had grown extremely tense, and the Soviets had stationed several army corps on Poland's border. And months later they would still be there.[5] A friendship pact with Poland would protect both Germany and the Poles from Russia, but first, Germany needed to regain from Poland some of the land it had lost at Versailles. If Hitler could not achieve that, he figured he could forget any alliance with them and subjugate the Poles.

* * *

The Poles were a proud people who had managed to retain their national character and unity through the one institution that still bound them together: the Roman Catholic Church. They were sensitive to the fact they had been the vassals of Germany, Austria, and Russia for 150 years and were determined to never again be ruled by another country.

Besides reestablishing the nation itself, one of the most important things Versailles had done for Poland was give it access to the Baltic Sea by creating a corridor through Prussia. The Polish Corridor was one hundred miles deep and anywhere from twenty to seventy miles across at any given point. On the Baltic, at the corridor's north end, were two ports. One was the former German port of Danzig, which the treaty had made a free city and now was overseen by the League of Nations. Danzig sat on the east side of the corridor, bordering East Prussia. Just a few miles west of it was the city of Gdynia, which the Poles had been building into an even greater port than Danzig.

Danzig included scores of towns and villages outside the city itself. Most of its inhabitants were German, and encouraged by Nazi agitators, they loudly demanded their return to the fatherland. So strong was their resentment they had put the Nazis in control of their government in 1935.

So on October 24, 1938, Ribbentrop, on Hitler's orders, met with Polish ambassador Józef Lipski over lunch at the Grand Hotel in Berchtesgaden and made a request. Germany wanted to create a corridor of its own across the Polish Corridor, a railroad, and an autobahn, the model for modern America's Interstate Highway System. And he wanted Danzig returned to the Reich. For its part, Poland would have free access to the port of Danzig, and it would of course continue to use its own port of Gdynia.[6] Hitler thought it a reasonable arrangement. So did the British, who were highly sympathetic to the demands of Danzig's Germans that they be returned to Germany.[7]

But the Polish government was dominated by three colonels, one of them its foreign minister, Józef Beck, and they balked. For one thing, the Vistula River, a major corridor through Poland, connected the port to the country's inland markets, including cities such as Warsaw. The river and the port of Danzig were critical conduits for Poland's foreign commerce. In addition, Poland was uncomfortable giving Germany autonomy over the strip of land Hitler wanted. Conceivably, it could enable Hitler to interfere with Poland's contact with Danzig and Gdynia. Despite the fact most of Danzig's inhabitants were German, Beck told Lipski, "Everything in Danzig is definitely bound up with Poland." Moreover, he insisted, the Treaty of Versailles had guaranteed Poland unrestricted access to Danzig.[8]

But Hitler persisted.

Beck was an inveterate gambler, and the following January, Hitler invited him to stop off at the Berghof on his way home from the tables of Monte Carlo. The führer used the occasion to again tell him that he wanted Danzig returned, saying, "Danzig is German, will always remain German, and will sooner or later become part of Germany." He insisted again that the autobahn and the railroad be built across the corridor. Beck was unbending, replying that Poland would need to control any such road and that Danzig would never be returned to Germany.[9]

Ribbentrop was rankled because Hitler received nothing from the Poles even though at Munich he had insisted that Poland be given part of Czechoslovakia.[10] At this point, Hitler still wanted to treat Poland gently and use the country as a buffer to protect Germany from the Soviet Union. Hitler believed Poland could be a friendly neighbor once he resolved the Danzig issue.

Shortly after Colonel Beck's visit to the Berghof, Ribbentrop journeyed to Warsaw in an attempt to turn the man around, but he got nowhere. Beck knew that handing over Danzig, as well as control of the mouth of the Vistula, would give the Germans power over Poland's economy, and that was out of the question. Beck did talk about helping Germany improve its communications with East Prussia. But so far as the autonomous corridor for the railroad and the highway was concerned, Beck said, Poland could never give Germany "sovereign rights" over any piece of Polish land.[11]

The visit did give Ribbentrop an inspiration. If Poland was so obstinate and therefore cool to a nonaggression pact, why not ally with Russia? That would solve the problem of securing an ally who could protect Germany's back. Moreover, it would enable Hitler to treat the Poles as he pleased.

In the coming months, Poland's leaders, under the delusion that their nation was a world power and need not bow to anyone, dug their heels in further. In early March, Hitler broke the commitment he had made at Munich and created a crisis in Czechoslovakia that prompted the country's ailing president, Emil Hácha, to meet with Hitler and Göring in Berlin. At the late-night session, Hitler bullied Hácha, announcing he would invade Czechoslovakia in mere hours, and Göring backed him by describing how he would bomb Hácha's beloved Prague. Hácha gave in and handed Hitler what remained of his country. Göring had been bluffing. He had told his wife, Emmy, the weather had been so bad he could not get his bombers off the ground, and his bullying of the old man haunted Göring long afterward. "I agree. It was not a gentlemanly thing to do," he often told Emmy.[12]

Four days later, on March 19, Hitler turned on Lithuania, which bordered Germany on the east and Poland to the north. He told the little state he would send in the Wehrmacht if it failed to hand over the port city of Memel, which had once belonged to Prussia. Lithuania quickly gave in, and Ribbentrop ignored the stormy reactions in the West. Less than two weeks after that, Ribbentrop and Hitler got a nasty surprise. On March 21, Britain approached the Polish government to suggest a mutual defense pact should the Germans attack the Poles.[13] The English would give Poland their support if Germany attacked Poland. To his utter shock, Hitler learned of the offer on March 31, when Neville Chamberlain announced it to the British Parliament. Six days later Beck visited London, and the two powers affirmed that they had concluded the agreement informally. It had not yet been signed but the British had given their word publicly.

The French added their promise as well.

The Abwehr, Germany's intelligence agency, learned of Britain's plan in advance, and when the agency's chief, Admiral Wilhelm Canaris, informed

Fig. 4.1. Hitler passes an honor guard as he arrives at the presidential castle in Prague on a wintery day in March 1939 and takes over the remainder of Czechoslovakia. General Keitel is on the far left.

the führer and warned that any moves against Poland would mean war, Hitler flew into a rage. He was so angry his face was distorted. He paced back and forth across the room, pounding on a marble tabletop and screaming threats. Finally, his eyes flashing, he growled, "I'll cook them in a stew that they'll choke on."[14]

The two Western powers had made an astounding commitment. Despite their belief that the Germans had a right to Danzig, Britain's leaders were now prisoners of their treaty, forced to keep their opinions about Danzig to themselves and support the Poles no matter what position Warsaw took. In essence, the pact gave Poland a blank check to drag Britain and France into war.

Not all Britons approved. "Never in her whole history has England ever left it to a second-class power to decide if she is to enter a war or not," Alfred Duff Cooper wrote in his diary. A member of Parliament, Duff Cooper had resigned from Chamberlain's cabinet the previous October in protest over the Munich compromise.[15]

The British had made the agreement believing the Polish army was strong, but in actuality, little of the army was mobilized. Even most of its cavalry still rode into battle on horses. And Poland's air force could not begin to compare with Germany's Luftwaffe.

Meanwhile, the Polish leaders remained dangerously overconfident. They believed the British, with their seasoned, well equipped armies and globe-straddling fleets, would force Hitler to back down. Besides, many people in Europe, including some key members of the British cabinet, did not believe Hitler would ever go to war.

Further emboldened, Poland informed Germany that it would not agree to Hitler's demands and that if the Germans tried to carry them out, it would mean war. Although the Poles had no hint of it, no sooner had Britain announced its pledge than Hitler ordered his general staff to prepare for the invasion of Poland on September 1—or any time before Poland's rainy season began and its dirt roads turned to mud.[16]

* * *

So far, the United States had, for the most part, kept out of the crisis. When Hitler had come to power, Franklin Roosevelt had appointed a University of Chicago history professor, William E. Dodd, ambassador to Berlin. Dodd had urged his bosses in Washington to take stands against the Nazis and their antisemitism, but the State Department had ignored him, and at the end of 1937, he had gone home in disgust.[17]

In September 1938, during the Munich crisis, Roosevelt had written Hitler and Mussolini, urging them to avoid war. Hitler had said little in response. And Roosevelt had remained quiet.

The president was under considerable pressure at home to stay out of the crisis. Like their French and British counterparts, many Americans had lost grievously in World War I and wanted no more foreign conflicts. The United States was beginning to profit from selling munitions to the British and French. The sales were helping turn around the US economy, but the public did not want further involvement. Moreover, some had sympathy for Hitler—in particular, a group of German descendants who had joined a pro-Nazi movement, the German American Bund. The Bund wore black-and-white uniforms similar to those of the Nazis, and to the dismay of many other Americans, their ranks had been multiplying.

On April 9, William C. Bullitt, Roosevelt's ambassador to France, reported that Georges-Étienne Bonnet, France's foreign minister, had asked him to tell Washington that "it was five minutes before twelve." War could come at any minute, Bullitt said.[18]

Five days later, Roosevelt sent a telegram to Hitler, asking for his assurance that the Wehrmacht would not attack a list of thirty nations. This time, Hitler responded with a flourish. He took Roosevelt's message to a session of the Reichstag, where he made fun of it almost line by line. Two of the states Roosevelt had asked him not to invade were former possessions of the Ottoman Empire—Syria and Palestine—and Hitler pointed out that under their peace agreement France and Britain had already taken over those lands. His audience responded with laughter and thunderous applause.[19]

* * *

While Ribbentrop and Hitler dealt with the Poles, a secret tug-of-war had been going on inside the Nazi hierarchy. For the past year, the leaders of Germany's military had been alarmed over Hitler's flirtation with war. In September 1938, at the height of the Sudeten crisis, a large group of Hitler's top officers had plotted to overthrow him if he tried to go to war. They intended to replace him by restoring Kaiser Wilhelm to the throne. Chamberlain's appeasement at Munich had stopped them.

The generals had good reason for their concerns. They all had experienced the horrors of World War I and wanted no more. Most important, they believed the armed forces were not prepared for a major conflict.[20] During World War I, Hitler the corporal had lost some of his vision in a gas attack and therefore should have been more wary. Yet Hitler disdained the generals, as he did anyone who did not share his views, and looked at them as weak aristocrats. Moreover, having an incredible ego, Hitler was convinced that he was such a political genius he could bluff the British and French into acquiescence.

Into the summer of 1939, the officers maintained their belief that a hard line toward Britain was not the answer. They thought running the risk of war foolhardy. The generals' link to Hitler was Wilhelm Keitel, a jaunty man who was chief of the Oberkommando der Wehrmacht, the high command of all the armed forces. Unlike most other officers, who came from Prussian military families, Keitel was from a family of well-to-do landowners in the eastern state of Hanover, where the Prussians were disliked. Taller than Hitler and most of the others, he had become the führer's yes-man in the military, always willing to do whatever Hitler desired. Thus, outside of Hermann Göring, Keitel was the one military leader who talked to Hitler regularly, and he tried to convince the führer that the generals had good reason to be concerned. Hitler tried to soothe them all by telling Keitel the plans they were drawing up for war against Poland were strictly defensive. They would go to war only if the Poles attacked Germany.[21]

Some civilians in the government advocated a peaceful approach as well. Many were career diplomats in the foreign office, but the most notable of them was Joseph Goebbels, a Nazi Party member from the early days who loudly proclaimed his hatred of the Jews. His height stunted, Goebbels had a clubfoot and a lust for beautiful actresses, who were easy to find since he controlled the film industry. Goebbels was a radical Nazi—a fanatic— and his espousal of a softer approach to the Poles astounded many. Most of the members of Hitler's entourage of lunch and dinner companions viewed Goebbels and the others who warned against war as men who had become rich being Nazi leaders and feared that war would take away their opulent lifestyles.[22]

One of those men was one of Hitler's closest confidants, Reichsmarschall Hermann Göring, who commanded the world's most formidable air force, the Luftwaffe. Göring was locked in a battle with Von Ribbentrop for Hitler's ear as he tried to persuade der führer that the British were losing patience and would go to war for the Poles if Germany attacked.

Göring and Ribbentrop were the same age and came from similar backgrounds. Ribbentrop's father had been an army officer and Göring's a diplomat. Göring was easy to know, a man who made friends readily, while Ribbentrop was humorless and had become what one of his childhood friends termed "a stuffed shirt." Some old friends now referred to him as "Ribbensnob."[23]

Göring had always thought Ribbentrop overrated. When Hitler had appointed the Champagne Salesman ambassador to London, Fat Boy urged him to reconsider, saying Ribbentrop's knowledge of foreign countries was limited. "Ribbentrop knows France only through champagne and England only through whiskey," Göring had told the führer.[24]

As Ribbentrop told Hitler that the British did not have the backbone to stand up to him, Göring warned Hitler to be cautious. He knew Britain was far more dangerous than Hitler realized. Göring, like most other Germans, wanted to retrieve the lands Germany had lost to the Poles, even if it meant invading Poland. Yet he believed Germany did not need to go to battle with the British to achieve that end, and if Germany did, the conflict would escalate into another world war, which the nation inevitably would lose. Göring had good reason to take that stand, for his duties included the oversight of Germany's armaments makers.[25]

An exceedingly intelligent man, Göring had been a World War I fighter ace in Baron Manfred von Richthofen's famous Flying Circus, one of history's most illustrious groups of fighter pilots. When Richthofen was shot down, Göring succeeded him as leader of the circus.

He had been attracted to the Nazi Party, as had many Germans, because he wanted the penalties of Versailles overturned and believed that the Nazis composed the only party that could do it. An early party member, he was one of Hitler's most loyal followers. In fact, he had marched beside Hitler in the 1923 Beer Hall Putsch, the Nazis' ill-fated attempt to overthrow the Bavarian government. During the march, Göring had been shot in the groin, and his wound was so painful he became addicted to the morphine his doctors gave him.[26]

The Treaty of Versailles banned Germany from having an air force, but when the Nazis came to power, Göring used Germany's fledgling airline, Lufthansa, as a cover to create the Luftwaffe. Göring also became interior minister of the state of Prussia and used the post to establish a secret intelligence service that monitored the telephones of a variety of people, including foreign ambassadors, fellow members of the German hierarchy, and even his own wife.[27]

Although disliked by many of the nation's other military leaders, Göring was highly popular with the German people. Yet he had a notable weakness: a craving for riches and ostentation. He used Nazi Party funds and the state treasury of Prussia to amass an incredible art collection and a gold-plated mansion on Berlin's Leipziger Platz. He also built a chalet near Hitler's home on the Obersalzberg and a lavish hunting lodge named Carinhall outside Berlin, where he displayed his collection of old masters that the Nazis had seized from Jewish families in Germany and later from museums in occupied countries.[28] So Hitler's dinner companions had cause to say that war could destroy Göring's lifestyle.

Göring was no angel. The American psychologist at the Nuremberg trials deemed him a psychopath.[29] As the Nazi leader of the state of Prussia, Göring had established the Gestapo, a secret police unit whose mission was to monitor enemies. Later, under the reichsmarschall's successor, Heinrich Himmler, the Gestapo became infamous for torturing and murdering those who disagreed with the Nazis, as well as Jews, gypsies, and others considered non-Aryan.

Göring was an ebullient man who was full of show and at times a brag-gart. He liked medals—so much so that he would maneuver to have some foreign government award him one. Göring loved the good life, dining on only the greatest cuisines. This lifestyle and his morphine addiction—which he tried to kick—had made Göring very fat.

Nevertheless, Göring was not all bad. He had a number of friends abroad, especially in Sweden, the homeland of his first wife. Although he, too, blamed the British for the economic woes the Treaty of Versailles had inflicted on Germany, Göring was an admirer of the British royal family. He had been scheduled to represent Germany at the coronation of King George VI but had to back off after Ribbentrop informed Hitler that a member of Parliament was opposing his appearance. It was most unfor-tunate, because in London, Göring was supposed to have met with Win-ston Churchill, who could have confirmed the reichsmarschall's concerns about war.[30]

With the new Anglo-Polish alliance, Poland's intransigence, and Hit-ler's order to draw up invasion plans, everyone had gone too far. Hitler was dealing with men like himself—tough talkers who gambled. The Brit-ish and the French were betting that Hitler would never invade Poland. An inveterate gambler himself, Józef Beck persuaded other Polish lead-ers that Britain and France would scare Hitler away. For his part, Hitler, urged on by Ribbentrop, bet that the British would back off as they had over Czechoslovakia.

All this dismayed Hermann Göring, who viewed the Poles as reckless and unyielding. To him, their pacts with Britain and France had made the Poles cocky and ready to take on Germany in a war that they mistakenly believed they would win.[31] As Ribbentrop's influence over Hitler seemed to grow, Göring's frustration mounted. "There is no need for war. Why don't these fools realize it?" he would tell his Swedish stepson. "If only the führer would leave it to me, I would see that Germany had her place in the sun and peace for a generation—but without war."[32]

Göring soon was offered an opportunity to do something. Among the reichsmarschall's foreign acquaintances was a Swedish engineer named Birger Dahlerus, who had befriended Göring's stepson.[33] Dahlerus had spent the early part of his career as a common workman in England, and as he rose in industry, the Swede came to know some of Britain's business and social leaders. All this had led him to develop a high respect for the tenacity of the English people and their unwavering loyalty to one another.[34]

In early summer of 1939, Dahlerus spent an evening with some of those acquaintances discussing the emerging crisis over Poland. Some English business leaders—fearful of the Communists like some of the aristocracy were—favored the Nazis. But from his talks that evening, Dahlerus found that those influential British business leaders were fed up with Germany and ready to stand firm against the Nazi regime. Concerned, Dahlerus believed he might be able to use his contacts to bring the two sides together.[35]

Two days later, he called on Göring at Carinhall, his estate outside Berlin. When Dahlerus relayed his findings, Göring was skeptical, saying the British wanted only to hold Germany down, but he agreed to meet with some of the Swede's English friends.[36] The secret meeting on August 7 at a private home in southern Sweden went exceedingly well, and everyone left convinced that talks between Göring and senior members of the British government might resolve the Polish crisis.[37]

Ribbentrop, who opposed his competitor's contact with Dahlerus, had been making moves since early April that threatened Göring's plans. Following up on his scheme for an alliance with the Russians, Ribbentrop had begun sending feelers out to the Soviet Union.

The Russians seemed surprisingly receptive to his overtures. They had been trying unsuccessfully to negotiate a mutual defense alliance with the English and French. For six years, Soviet premier Josef Stalin had sought a treaty so that Russia would have some form of protection from Germany, but the Soviet foreign office's attempts had been so unsuccessful he had fired his foreign minister, Maxim Litvinov, in early May. Almost immediately, the new foreign minister, Vyacheslav Molotov, persuaded the British and French to discuss a mutual assistance alliance. The French were receptive, but Britain's Neville Chamberlain was cool to any dealings with the godless Communists. Once again, Chamberlain demonstrated his naïvete by ignoring the strategic advantage the pact would have given Britain over Germany.

The British continued to stall until late July, when they and the French dispatched diplomats to Moscow to discuss the idea, but again, they seemed resistant to action. At that point, Stalin lost patience and authorized Molotov to open up to the German overtures. If they could not get an agreement with the angels, they would see about a pact with the devil himself.[38]

Thus, on the night of August 21, while Hitler was at dinner in the Berghof, an aide handed him a note. He scanned it and stared off for a moment. Then he banged his fist down on the table so hard it rattled the glasses and startled his companions. Throwing his hands over his head, he declared excitedly, "I have them! I have them!" But he gave no explanation to anyone, and in seconds, he regained his composure and resumed eating while the rest in the room sat bewildered. No one dared ask what was going on, but afterward, Hitler took the men into another room and told them he had received a note from Stalin agreeing to discuss a pact. German radio announced that Ribbentrop would leave for Moscow the next day to draft the agreement.[39]

* * *

Two days later, on August 23, Göring was to go to England on a secret mission to meet with Britain's prime minister, Neville Chamberlain. So that no one would recognize him, Göring was to fly to a private airfield near the prime minister's official country home, Chequers. To further insure secrecy, Chamberlain had sent the household staff on leave, and members of the British secret service had taken over their duties. When the news of Stalin's message reached him, Ribbentrop lost no time telling Hitler that there was no longer a need for Göring to make the trip. Hitler agreed and withdrew his approval of Göring's venture.[40]

Britain's leaders heard the announcement of Ribbentrop's trip from Berlin radio, and they were shocked. To them, any alliance with the Soviets was theirs to make. In their eyes, the advantage Germany would gain from this treaty was potentially a hostile act. Nevertheless, Chamberlain waited expectantly through the next day for Göring. Always hopeful he still could sit down with Britain's leaders, the reichsmarschall never notified London that he was postponing his trip. Two days later, after the pact with Russia had been cemented with signatures, the Germans told the British that, by order of the führer, Göring would not be coming. After the war, Göring said Ribbentrop's "dirty trick" was "probably decisive for history."[41]

5

"CLOSE YOUR HEARTS TO PITY!"

M<small>EANWHILE, IN EARLY</small> A<small>UGUST</small> 1939, H<small>ITLER ATTEMPTED TO</small> short-cut the concerns of his top military commanders by inviting their chiefs of staff to the Berghof, where he laid out his arguments for a tough stand against Poland. England, he assured them, might talk big and might even call home its ambassador or embargo trade with Germany, but the country would never go to war for Poland.[1] It did not work. The generals were notably unresponsive. One officer asked questions that challenged Hitler's reasoning, and the others sat in silence. Hitler came away bitter.[2] His only option was to assemble all the commanders for a pep talk at the Berghof.

Midmorning on August 22, a steady stream of cars began making the hard right turn off the road from Berchtesgaden and drove up to the foot of a long stone staircase broad enough for five men. Inside the cars were the leaders of Germany's army, navy, and air force. To keep their presence secret, all had been ordered to wear civilian clothes.[3]

Each man stepped out, climbed the stairs, and strode into a long hallway with arched ceilings. Turning into a doorway on their right, they all entered the Berghof's great hall. It was a monumental room, designed to awe any visitor, no matter how important or powerful he or she might be. The chamber was roughly seventy feet long and forty feet wide, and the far end was dominated by a massive window that could be lowered by an electric motor and that provided a panoramic view of the mountains in Austria across the nearby border. In front of the window stood a table, and facing the table were rows of chairs where the men were to sit.

They walked down three wide steps of marble that divided the room. To right and left hung Gobelin tapestries. Overhead, heavy oak beams stretched from wall to wall, and a low wainscoting ran all around the walls.

Above that paneling hung six paintings by Italian and German artists, among them a pristine Italian Madonna and a lush nude.

Included in the assemblage were the leaders of all the German armed forces that faced the Polish border. Erich Raeder, commander of the navy and its fleet of U-boats, led a complement of admirals. Keitel led the generals. Chief of the army general staff Franz Halder, a Bavarian and the son of a general, was also there. All the generals looked stern and forbidding, but Halder appeared all the more so wearing his pince-nez. Another was army commander in chief Walther von Brauchitsch, an affable Prussian aristocrat. Like many others in the aristocracy, Von Brauchitsch had no use for the Nazis.

Probably the most esteemed of the generals was Gerd von Rundstedt, commander of Army Group South, which had been moved to Poland's border under the guise of maneuvers. Von Rundstedt, a charming man who made little secret of his disdain for the Nazis and saw Hitler as nothing more than a mentally impaired corporal, came from an ancient line of Prussian officers. The general had served in the army for forty-seven years. Von Rundstedt was uncomfortable in his civvies that day, complaining they were "a funny disguise."[4]

One of the later arrivals was a thin, prematurely gray man of fifty-seven, Admiral Wilhelm Canaris, who headed the Abwehr, Germany's intelligence service. Although a conservative, Canaris also disliked the Nazis. Two of his Abwehr subordinates had organized the plot to overthrow Hitler during the Munich crisis, and he, Brauchitsch, and Halder had been among the leaders. He stood unobtrusively in the back of the hall, and although everyone had been instructed not to take any notes, Canaris and Halder—sitting with the other generals—took down all that Hitler said.

One of the last to enter the room was Hermann Göring, who strode past the others and took a seat beside Hitler's conference table. Usually resplendent in his blue reichsmarschall's uniform, today he wore the lederhosen of a Bavarian huntsman—a green jacket with large yellow buttons, gray shorts, and gray silk stockings—and, around his huge waist, a red sword belt with inlaid gold, an ornamental dagger hanging in a matching red-and-gold holder.[5] The bizarre costume, which he usually wore at Obersalzberg, only emphasized Göring's huge body, and the shorts showed off his pudgy legs. Few of the officers there liked him, and Erich von Manstein, Rundstedt's chief of staff, leaned over to the general next to him and said, "I suppose the Fat Boy's here as a strong-arm man?"[6]

The officers began their meeting at ten o'clock, discussing the directives Hitler had given for the invasion. They went through the unconventional tactics Hitler insisted they use. It would be what they called a *lightning war*, a blitzkrieg. Armored divisions would encircle the Polish armies, netting them in, while the infantry killed them or took them prisoner. There would be no prolonged trench war, as had happened to Hitler in World War I. With the blitzkrieg, they would overcome Poland in a matter of a few weeks.

While they met, Adolf Hitler waited directly above the great hall in his private suite, which consisted of two bedrooms and a study. One of the bedrooms belonged to Hitler's mistress, Eva Braun, whose connection with the führer was such a close secret that she had to remain out of sight when important visitors came to the Berghof. At one end of the suite was the study, a long bright room carpeted with undyed lamb's wool. Three of the study's walls were lined with blond paneling, and three windows stretched across the fourth wall, facing the same Alpine panorama that the large window of the great hall displayed.

As noon approached, all the lesser officers and the field commanders left the great hall, leaving only the high command, as well as the army and group commanders and their chiefs of staff. Now was the time for Hitler to make his pitch. Preceded by his bodyguards in their black uniforms, he strode into the great hall. The officers all jumped to attention, their right arms stretched out in the Hitler salute. The führer took his place standing behind the long table in front of the window. He faced a notable challenge. To rouse these men and make them believe in his invasion, he needed to use the same eloquence that had won over the German people. Some, like Von Rundstedt, would be an especially hard sell.

"I have called you together to give you a picture of the political situation," Hitler started. "After this, we shall discuss military details." Then he began making his case, his deep voice soft.

"It was clear to me that a conflict with Poland had to come sooner or later. I had already made this decision in the spring, but I thought that I would first turn against the west in a few years and only after that against the east."

Quickly, briskly, Hitler let the words roll, his voice cutting across the room as he grew louder and more commanding. "I wanted, first of all, to establish a tolerable relationship with Poland in order to fight first against the west," he said, but he added that if he were to do that, Poland could attack Germany.

Also, he said with his typical lack of modesty, his own presence made it imperative to strike promptly. "Essentially, all depends on me, on my existence, because of my political talents," he declared. "Probably no one will ever again have the confidence of the whole German people as I have. There will probably never again in the future be a man with more authority than I have. My existence is therefore a factor of great value, but it can be eliminated at any time by a criminal or a lunatic."

His next words must have sent chills down the spines of the generals who had plotted the year before, because Hitler made it plain he knew of their conversations with English friends at the time of their scheming. "It did much damage to us," he asserted.

He added that the presence of his ally, Italy's Benito Mussolini, also made this a timely moment because the Italian court opposed Il Duce. "If anything happens to him, Italy's loyalty to the alliance will no longer be certain," Hitler said.

The western powers, he declared, had no strong leaders like himself and Benito Mussolini. "There is no outstanding personality in England and France," he said. "We have no other choice. We must act," he told them. "Our opponents will be risking a great deal and can gain only a little. Britain's stake in a war is inconceivably great. Our enemies have leaders who are below average. No personalities, no masters, no men of action." Some of those officers must have remembered those words a year later, when Winston Churchill was rallying Britain against the Germans.

Hitler reminded everyone that he had built Germany's power and extended the country's boundaries with bluffs that did not test the real strength of the nation's war machine. "The use of military weapons is necessary before the final great showdown with the west," Hitler said. "It is necessary to test the military." He, too, opposed another world war, Hitler assured them, claiming that this invasion would be merely a local conflict.

"The relationship with Poland has become unbearable!" he declared again, increasing his tempo with a series of short, quick sentences, his arm swinging down and his hand punctuating each sentence like an exclamation point. "Poland changed her tone toward us! A permanent state of tension is intolerable! The power of initiative cannot be allowed to pass to others! The present moment is more favorable than in two or three years' time!" he said. "One cannot forever face one another with rifles cocked!"

He grew more eloquent, reminding everyone of the bluffs he had won. "I have always taken a great risk in the conviction that it would succeed," he said. "Now it is also a great risk. Iron nerves, iron resolution!"

As he flung out each new point, Hitler paused a moment, surveying his audience. Whenever he turned his head, the crisp light from the window behind him seemed to sharpen his pointed nose, and with each new statement, each new argument, his face, like his hand, seemed to capture his listeners.

Hitler declared that Britain was weak willed. "She will not take any risks," he said. France as well, he added. Therefore, he assured them, "military intervention is out of the question." Ignoring the possibility that Britain might not back down, Hitler declared, "It is nonsense to say that England wants to wage a long war." But some of the officers kept thinking, *Britain could do it nonetheless.*

Now with the new pact with Russia, he claimed, there would be nothing to fear from the east. In fact, if the British blockaded Germany as they had in World War I, the Reich would have ample food supplies from the Soviet Union. "The enemy did not reckon with my great strength of purpose. Our enemies are small fry. I saw them at Munich."

"Now!" he cried triumphantly. "Poland is in the position in which I wanted her!"

With studied deliberateness, Hitler spat out the words as he wound up to his finale. The Germans were embarking on a great task, and it called for great efforts, he said. "A start has been made on the destruction of England's hegemony. The ways will be open for the soldiers after I have made the political preparations." He concluded, "The effect on Poland will be tremendous," and as his voice trailed off, the officers jumped to their feet. As was the custom, Hermann Göring thanked him on behalf of everyone, saying he could count on them.

It was nearly two in the afternoon, time for lunch.

Once fed, all the officers settled back into the semicircle of chairs. So far, they had seemed unresponsive. Taking his place again behind the table, Hitler began, acknowledging he could not prophesy precisely what Britain and France would do but predicted relations would be severed between Germany and the two western powers. He expected a trade embargo but no blockade, yet Germany needed to stand fast, he said, and his voice continued to rise as he tried to stir the officers. They needed to keep building Germany's western defense wall, and they all needed to display "iron steadfastness." There would be no shrinking from anything, Hitler declared.

Turning now to Poland, he informed his officers that their goal was not to reach a certain point on the map or to create a new German border but to destroy Poland's armed forces. "Even if war breaks out in the west," he said, "the destruction of Poland remains the priority."

The way the war started would make no difference, he said, trying to reassure them. "I shall give a propagandist reason for starting the war, no matter whether it is plausible or not," he added. "The victor will not be asked afterwards whether he told the truth or not. When starting and waging a war, it is not right that matters but victory."

Few there knew it, but when he talked of "a propagandist reason" for the invasion, Hitler was referring to a plot he had assigned to the SS, the same military arm that was guarding him outside.

His voice rising, Hitler urged the officers to be unflinchingly brutal. They would need to wage the war harshly. "Close your hearts to pity!" he cried. "Act brutally! Eighty million people must obtain what is their right!"

Then his voice softened, and he went into brief details about the armies' first missions, instructing that they use Germany's technical superiority to shatter the Poles' nerves. The panzer divisions were to encircle the Polish units, cutting them off from any support. If the Poles regrouped, they would have to put them down again.

Then, to everyone's surprise, Hitler announced that they would launch the attack in just five days, that Saturday morning, August 26, rather than September 1, the date he had given them in the spring.

With that, he had each senior commander stand and describe the part his men were supposed to play. Already well versed in all the details of the invasion, Hitler frequently interrupted to add innovations of his own.

When the last officer finished, Hitler walked out, and the officers prepared to return to Berlin or their various field headquarters along the Polish border.[7] The news of the Russian pact made many feel that the Poles would recognize that their situation was hopeless and that Hitler had planned for the contents of their meeting to leak out, causing the British and Poles to give in. Thus, if he won the bluff, there would be no war.[8]

* * *

As Hitler walked out, he signaled for Göring, Keitel, Brauchitsch, and Halder to follow. Once alone, Hitler confided to the four that he was concerned about the two western nations—something he had not mentioned when

Map 5.1. The Polish corridor (*upper right*) separated the remainder of Germany from East Prussia and gave Poland access to the Baltic Sea.

trying to stir up the others. Despite his assurances to the generals, he said, there could be war with Britain and France. He wanted Poland vanquished swiftly, he explained, because then the other two nations would face a fait accompli that would pressure them to talk peace.

It probably was after the three officers had left when Hitler told Göring he could not fly off to see Chamberlain the next day. Göring reminded Hitler that his friend Birger Dahlerus had already established an unofficial line of communication between the reichsmarschall and the group of British business leaders. Perhaps, suggested Göring, Dahlerus could become his own unofficial connection to the British government, thereby enabling him to woo England away from the Poles.

That swung Hitler back toward Göring's side. This could be an answer to his private worries. After all, he must have reasoned, this would do no harm, and it might dissuade the two powers from acting.

Göring said he would invite Dahlerus to Berlin the next day, and he and the führer discussed the proposal they would have the Swede convey to London.[9]

6

A PERFORMANCE OF BOMBAST
AND THREATS

HITLER'S MEALS WERE ALMOST A CEREMONY. THE FÜHRER never dined early, and the table was always filled with guests, whose seating he personally directed. The guests were members of a clinging band of followers, a collection of people who depended on Hitler's good humor just as fervently as his ego demanded their presence.[1] Hitler always took over the table talk, and it was boring—so much so that many learned to stay away and avoid it altogether. "Hitler's conversations were monologues," Otto Dietrich said. "They were characterized by endless digressions and repetitions of the same basic ideas."[2]

Dinner was well along on the evening of August 22, and as usual, Hitler was dominating the conversation. But around ten o'clock in the evening, it all was interrupted when an aide informed him that Sir Nevile Henderson, the British ambassador, was asking for an audience, and the führer got up and went into another room.

Henderson had told the German foreign office in Berlin that he had a personal message for Hitler from Prime Minister Neville Chamberlain. More than that, the office reported that the British cabinet had met that afternoon and had reaffirmed its support of Poland. Worse yet, the cabinet had ordered that Britain's mobilization be stepped up.

Hitler was most surprised. Rather than news of the Russian talks cowering them, the English were showing strength that he and Ribbentrop had never expected. Unless it was a bluff so that London could wrest back the initiative Hitler had gained from the Russian talks, this did not indicate weakness.

Hitler had the Berghof operator reach Baron Ernst von Weizsäcker, the foreign office's state secretary who was in charge while Ribbentrop was away. Hoping he could delay the meeting until the talks had ended in Moscow, Hitler inquired of the baron whether a head of state could receive an ambassador when his foreign minister was absent. The baron was well seasoned in the art of diplomacy, having served in the foreign service since 1920. Moreover, he had no love for his boss, Ribbentrop, and opposed his hard line with England. Weizsäcker replied that Hitler certainly could receive Henderson. His rank and the current state of affairs, the baron added, made it imperative that Hitler meet with him.

Hitler ordered Weizsäcker to see whether Henderson would wait until Ribbentrop returned. Soon Weizsäcker called back, reporting that Henderson insisted that he could not wait. London wanted him to deliver the letter to Hitler personally—and as quickly as possible. Fearing that the letter might contain some proposal that, if made public, would upset Ribbentrop's talks in Moscow, Hitler ordered Weizsäcker to find out from Henderson whether the letter included any settlement terms or concrete proposals. He also requested Weizsäcker to tell Henderson that he was concerned because only the year before, someone had leaked to the press a private letter to him—a blatant lie. In addition, Hitler instructed the baron to tell the ambassador that he would give him an answer about their meeting early in the morning.

When Weizsäcker called back, he said Henderson had replied that he knew of no such leak and that there was no plan to make this letter public, thus calling Hitler's bluff. Apparently, the state secretary reported, the letter contained nothing damaging. It declared, first, that Britain was determined to stand by its pledge to Poland and, second, that if there was no longer the threat of war, England was ready to discuss all the issues that separated it from Germany. Third, Weizsäcker reported, the letter proposed that while Germany and Britain talked, Poland and Germany might also discuss their differences.

Although he might have softened a bit and had allowed Göring to communicate with the British, Hitler was determined to gain all he demanded of the Poles, even at the threat of war. So, since the letter did not seem to put Hitler in a position in which he would be forced to negotiate, he agreed to see Henderson. But, he said, he would keep the conversation focused only on his complaint that Germans living in Poland were being mistreated. He planned to end the meeting after only five minutes.

Then he informed Ribbentrop, who had stopped overnight in Königs-berg, in East Prussia, on his way to Moscow. Still convinced the Germans could cower the English, Ribbentrop pushed Hitler to be belligerent and tough and to make it hard on Henderson. Always jealous of anyone who had the führer's ear, Ribbentrop was furious that Hitler had sought Weizsäck-er's advice—so much so that he called the state secretary, woke him, and lambasted him for talking with Hitler.

The next morning, August 23, a disappointed Göring flew to Berlin rather than England, and at ten thirty, he called Dahlerus in Stockholm. The situation had turned for the worse, and war had become much more likely, he said before asking Dahlerus to come to Berlin.[3]

Meanwhile, Hitler's morning briefing was not going well. All the re-ports were overshadowed by details of the steps Britain had taken the pre-ceding afternoon. Contrary to Ribbentrop's assurances, the British public was in rebellion over the news that Chamberlain's foot-dragging had caused the Soviets to turn their backs on an alliance with England and make a pact with Hitler. The people demanded that the government take action and stand up to the Germans. There even was talk of forcing Chamberlain out.

Furthermore, on the other side of the globe, the Japanese, whom the Germans wanted as allies, were furious. Russia was Japan's historic enemy, and news of the pact caused such concern in Tokyo that there was talk of the government falling. If Hitler sought any union with the Japanese, this would not help.

Making matters worse, the Reich Foreign Office complained to the am-bassador from Tokyo that a Japanese correspondent, apparently using Ger-man sources, had reported that the Germans and the Russians had secretly agreed to divide Poland between themselves. Germany, he had written, would soon go to war against Poland, and neutralizing Russia would help. Indeed, Ribbentrop and the Russians were about to negotiate a protocol that would split eastern Europe into Soviet and German spheres of influ-ence. It was to be a secret appendix to their treaty.[4]

Hitler reacted by reaffirming what he had told the generals the day be-fore and ordering Colonel Schmundt, his chief military aide, to send Keitel his written order for the invasion at dawn the next Saturday, August 26.

That done, Hitler went downstairs to receive the British ambassador. It was a little after one in the afternoon. Henderson had flown down from Berlin with Weizsäcker. With them were an interpreter and Walther Hewel, who headed Ribbentrop's personal staff. An old friend of Hitler, Hewel had been one of the party's earliest members. The führer found the three men waiting in the great hall, where he had addressed his generals and admirals the preceding day, and the four men sat around the coffee table in front of the fireplace on the hall's upper level.

Looking like a Hollywood version of a British ambassador, Henderson was a tall, tweedy man who had a monocle dangling from his jacket. His suit contrasted with the dull brown of Hitler's party uniform, and a red carnation in Henderson's lapel presented a cheerier mood than that of the Iron Cross that hung over Hitler's left breast.

Speaking in German, Henderson thanked Hitler for receiving him so promptly. He could not have waited for Ribbentrop's return, he explained, because his government feared the situation was too critical for any delay.

Hitler glanced over a German translation of the letter the ambassador had brought. He coolly said he wanted to give Henderson a written reply— but first he wanted to say some things that would be along the lines of his note.

Trying to prevent Hitler from launching into one of his monologues, Henderson interrupted. He urged Hitler to read the prime minister's letter, not dwelling on past events but thinking of present and future situations. They could not undo the past, he argued. There could be no peace without Anglo-German cooperation.

Britain should have realized that a little sooner, Hitler snapped back, referring to England's treaty with Poland. He was warming up, following Ribbentrop's advice to be tough. He charged that the Polish problem would have been settled on the most generous terms if Britain had not given Poland its support. It was all the result of a British press campaign that falsely reported that Germany was threatening Poland.

The ambassador quickly replied that Britain had guaranteed to defend Poland if it were attacked and therefore needed to keep its word. Through the centuries, Britain had never gone back on its promises. It would not remain Great Britain if it did now. Britain had given its guarantees to Poland, and, he warned, now she must honor them.

"Then honor them," Hitler replied. "If you have given a blank check, you must also meet it!" Germany was in no way responsible for any guarantees the British might hand out, but the English would be responsible for the consequences of those promises. He growled that England should understand this and realize it clearly.

Hitler poured it on, growing more excited and less compromising. His words were tough and even violent, and his claims were often wild. Launching into his planned tirade on the minority problem, Hitler declared that any further persecution of Germans living in Poland would bring about Germany's immediate retribution. Noting Britain's mobilization, he claimed that Germany's preparations in comparison were purely defensive. "If I should hear of further measures of this sort being taken by England today or tomorrow," he thundered, "I shall immediately order general mobilization in Germany!"

War would then be inevitable, Henderson replied with an air of finality.

The English were always talking about the "poisoned atmosphere" that shrouded European affairs, but the English themselves poisoned the atmosphere, Hitler said. Then he launched back into his claims that the German minority was being persecuted. They were being dragged off to concentration camps and driven from their homes, he charged, as if the Nazis were not doing precisely that to Jews and people who disagreed with them.

German institutions were being shut down, he continued. And the Poles were castrating German men.

In a quiet voice, Henderson interrupted him. He had heard of only one such case, and that German had been a "sex maniac" who had deserved his punishment.

There had been six cases of castration, Hitler countered—once again stretching the truth. Britain's treaty with Poland was to blame for all the persecution, he added. England had given Poland a blank check to do all this. Now, he said, England had to pay, and Germany had to take a firm stand.

When Henderson replied that Germany had forced Britain to give Poland the guarantee, Hitler only went into another tirade.

The two men sparred, Hitler making wild claims and accusations, Henderson disputing them with facts. Desperately, Henderson tried to convince Hitler that Britain was serious and would go to war if need be. But Hitler did not believe him, and he bluffed with threats and false claims, thinking London would wilt and back down.

England, Hitler said, had made an enemy of the very man who wanted to be its greatest friend. England was to come to know a Germany that was quite different from the one it had imagined for so many years.

England knew Germany was strong, Henderson quickly responded, but Britain was determined to honor its obligations to Poland.

Now, Hitler said, if Poland made any further moves against the German nationals or against the Nazi regime in the free city of Danzig, he would intervene immediately. And any mobilization in the west would be answered by mobilization in Germany.

"Is that a threat?" Henderson asked quietly.

"No, a protective measure!" Hitler said.

The British government had made cooperation with Germany second to everything else, Hitler charged. They even had tried to make a pact with Russia.

Henderson pointed out that it was Germany who was making the alliance with the Soviets.

He was forced to do so, Hitler insisted, because England and France wanted to destroy him.

Not true, Henderson said. British public opinion had turned against Germany after Hitler's takeover of Czechoslovakia.

Then Hitler changed his tactics and turned warm and friendly, trying to use charm and telling Henderson that he was not blaming him personally. Henderson's attempts to promote friendship between the two countries were very much appreciated in Berlin, Hitler said.

Picking up on that cue, the ambassador noted that any German action against Poland would bring war and that would be a true tragedy.

Should war come, Hitler warned, it would be a battle of life and death. Picking up on what he had told the generals, he added that while Germany would have nothing to lose from a war, Britain would lose much. He did not want a war, he said, but he would not shrink from one if it proved necessary.

"People in England have tried to make out that I was bluffing last September," Hitler said. "They were absolutely wrong. I can assure you that I was not bluffing then any more than I am bluffing now."

While it is easy to foresee the beginning of a war, no one can foretell a war's course or how it ends, the ambassador warned. Early victories do not mean a final victory.

Hitler complained again that Britain had taken a stand against Germany, and Henderson countered that it was because Germany had threatened to use force. Yet, the ambassador added, he still believed they could come to a peaceful agreement. Why not Germany reestablish its talks with the Poles?

After a bit more of this, Hitler told Henderson he would have a response to Chamberlain's note in two hours. Henderson replied that he would go back to Salzburg and wait, the two men shook hands, and Henderson walked out. Unfortunately, Henderson had chosen to speak in German, a language in which he was by no means as proficient as a German interpreter would have been, thereby omitting important subtleties and nuances that the interpreter would have conveyed.

When the door to the great hall had closed behind him, Hitler slapped his thigh and laughed. This, he was hoping, would add to the prime minister's problems. "Chamberlain won't survive that conversation. His cabinet will fall this evening," he told Hewel and Weizsäcker. Not necessarily so, Weizsäcker said. The British were such prisoners of their own policy that they would not get out of their guarantee to Poland. Chamberlain would not fall, he predicted. Instead, the prime minister would gain all of Parliament behind him, and they would stand firm against the Germans.

After dictating his note to Chamberlain, Hitler went off to lunch, where he began pondering Weizsäcker's warning. The state secretary had noticed that Hitler had difficulty making decisions. Like many politicians who spent their lives reacting to the mood of the public, Hitler could be swayed back and forth, finally deciding according to the person he had heard from last.

Weizsäcker's advice caused him to change his tack a little. He decided to hand the ambassador his note in person. They needed to talk again, he reasoned. He should allure Henderson rather than rant at him. He would be calm but as fatalistic and unrelenting as he had been earlier. Yet Weizsäcker had tried to warn him that tack would not change the British.

The little group sat together again around the coffee table in front of the great hall's fireplace, and Hitler handed the ambassador his reply to Chamberlain. It was an eight-point document that essentially repeated what Hitler had said to Henderson, including his threat to mobilize if the British and French went further.

The letter concluded by declaring that there could not be any change in the "spirit" between Germany and Britain until England and France agreed to revise the "dictate" of the Treaty of Versailles.

The ambassador began reading the document. When he came upon the passage that threatened mobilization, Henderson looked up and asked Hitler precisely what he meant. Hitler explained. That would be equivalent to war, Henderson replied.

Trying to avoid seeming belligerent, Hitler turned cryptic. If Britain and France continued to mobilize and it convinced him they planned to attack Germany, he would mobilize in self-defense, he answered.

Germany already was mobilized, said Henderson. Any move by the British would be nothing compared with the present state of Germany's army.

Henderson finally finished reading the note and looked at Hitler. He obviously was disappointed that Hitler had not softened his earlier stance. He regretted this message, Henderson said, his voice growing sad as he talked of the tragedy of war and the grave responsibility that lay on Hitler.

There were people in the British government who wanted war, Hitler responded quietly.

Not true, the ambassador said. Chamberlain had always been a friend of Germany. He even had excluded Germany's loudest critic, Winston Churchill, from his cabinet.

Turning on the charm, Hitler assured Henderson that he did not consider him personally an enemy of Germany. But Germany's relations with Britain had been a series of disappointments. Then, citing the conviction most Germans held that Britain had deliberately destroyed their economic prowess, Hitler declared that Britain was determined to exterminate Germany.

Such talk was absurd, Henderson said. Nations could not be exterminated, and a prosperous Germany was in Britain's best interest.

He himself had been a soldier, and he knew what war was like, Hitler said. He would use every means at his disposal when he waged war. This time, the Germans would fight to the last man. "At the next instance of Polish provocation, I shall act," he announced, his voice so cold and calm it sounded deadly. "The questions of Danzig and the corridor will be settled one way or another. Please take note of this."

War seemed inevitable, Henderson concluded, and he regretted that both his own mission to Berlin and this visit to Hitler had failed.

With that, Henderson stood and reached out. The two shook hands, and he left.[5]

* * *

Hitler's thoughts now turned to Italy. Hitler had always admired Benito Mussolini. It was a love affair between dictators. Hitler had modeled his Nazi Brownshirts after the Italian's semimilitary unit, the Blackshirts. Three years earlier, Germany and Italy had made a pact of mutual friendship, creating an alliance that Mussolini had labeled the Axis. After the British had promised to protect Poland the past spring, they had upgraded their alliance by signing the Pact of Steel, a military treaty that bound the Italians to go to war alongside Germany if the Germans entered into a conflict. At the time, Mussolini had assumed that any war would be three years away and not immediately, for Italy was not prepared.

Moreover, many of Mussolini's senior lieutenants were uneasy with the alliance. Their concerns had grown stronger on August 11, when Galeazzo Ciano, Italy's foreign minister, visited his German opposite at Fuschl, Ribbentrop's castle near Salzberg that the Nazis had confiscated from a political opponent. Ciano, who also was Mussolini's son-in-law, was taking a prelunch stroll in the castle's garden with Ribbentrop when he asked what exactly Germany wanted from Poland. "The corridor or Danzig?" As if dealing with some inconsequential office detail, Ribbentrop turned, looked coldly at Ciano, and said, "Not anymore. We want war."[6]

Ten days later, before his departure, Ribbentrop had told the Italians he was going to Moscow, but there had been no communication since, making Rome more uneasy. The Italians were temperamental people, and as Hitler had said to his generals the day before, the Roman court was opposed to Mussolini. It would not welcome any suggestion that the country support Germany's attack on Poland. Hitler realized he should woo Mussolini more if he hoped to have Italy with him. If Italy failed to link arms with Germany, it would be yet more difficult to bully Britain and France into backing down.

Hitler therefore instructed Weizsäcker to call Ciano, Mussolini's foreign minister, and let him know that Henderson had just left and that Hitler had been hard and unbending with him. As Ciano was already trying to avoid war and worried about the events in Moscow, Weizsäcker's news failed to win the Italian. Ciano hung up even more downhearted.[7]

Hitler then began his usual five o'clock press briefing upstairs in his study, where he was interrupted by a telephoned cable from Ribbentrop in Moscow. The talks were going well, he reported, but the Russians were making trouble over the secret protocol to divide eastern Europe into spheres of influence. As Hitler had instructed, Ribbentrop had offered the Soviets all of Finland and parts of the Baltic states of Estonia and Latvia. But the Russians also wanted two cities in Latvia, the ports of Libau and Windau. Hitler had wanted to retain the remaining lands for Germany, so Ribbentrop asked what he should do. The agreement was too crucial to him to quibble over such a pittance, and Hitler instructed his foreign minister to give them what they asked.[8]

The pact would soon be signed, and Hitler now was free to act. But, he wondered, would Britain back down or go to war? Had his performance for Henderson been convincing? And he was especially worried whether Mussolini would give his crucial support.

Late that evening, Hitler was standing on the Berghof's broad terrace with some of his guests. He began pacing back and forth with his Luftwaffe adjutant, Nicolas von Below, asking the colonel about the strength of the Polish air force. The sky to the north was a strange color, turquoise from a display of northern lights, or aurora borealis, and slowly it began to turn violet, then bloodred. The two stood and gazed up.

This, Von Below said to Hitler, seemed a forecast of a bloody war.

If it must be, the sooner the better, Hitler said, adding that the longer the delay the bloodier the war would be.[9]

About the same time in Moscow, Ribbentrop and the Russians were signing their agreement.

7

"A SECOND BISMARCK"

THE FOLLOWING MORNING, HITLER FRETTED OVER ITALY'S POSITION. He was calmer—and much less certain, now even inviting suggestions from Weizsäcker and admitting to the state secretary how uneasy he was.

His doubts were well founded, Weizsäcker replied. The Pact of Steel bound the countries to not only aid each other in times of war but also keep each other informed. Now, Weizsäcker said, the Italians were acting as if the Polish crisis did not involve them at all. He had learned from Ciano's brother-in-law that Italy would refuse to give any aid to the Germans if Hitler went to war over Poland. The brother-in-law, Count Magistrati, was counselor of the Italian embassy in Berlin. If war came, he had told Weizsäcker, they would declare the Pact of Steel void because the Germans had failed to consult them on the progress of the crisis. England would help Poland, Weizsäcker warned Hitler, but Italy would not help Germany.

Not only that, Weizsäcker reported, but just that morning, he had received a letter from Hans Georg von Mackensen, Germany's ambassador to Rome, and he handed it to the führer, saying it generally confirmed what Magistrati had said. Hitler put on his rimless spectacles, their lenses thick, and looked at the letter. Not only did it confirm the count's warning—Mackensen also reported that Italy was unable to finance a war and its armed forces were ill equipped for one.

Moreover, the ambassador said, Mussolini had ordered Ciano to meet as soon as possible with Ribbentrop and make it plain that their treaty with Germany required that Hitler not go to war unless the Italians agreed. The Italians' mood was yet more rebellious, Mackensen reported. Mussolini had instructed his foreign minister to be guided by the watchword "Friends and allies, yes! Slaves, no!" He had given Ciano those instructions before Germany had announced its pact with the Soviets, Mackensen said. Hitler recalled that Ciano had tried to meet with Ribbentrop before the foreign minister had left for Moscow, and that, Hitler quickly reasoned, would explain what the Italian foreign minister had wanted.

Hitler read further. Now that Russia was friendly to Germany, the Italians believed that Poland had no choice but to negotiate with Hitler. Nevertheless, should the war come, Italy planned to offer its own "formula" for a solution, possibly something involving the Balkans, where Mussolini had been hoping to expand Italy's borders. Quite clearly, Mussolini was interested not in settling the dispute with Poland but in using the conflict to grab land for Italy. That notion discomforted Hitler, who sought only troops from Italy, not any "formula."

Taken aback, Hitler told Weizsäcker he wanted no war with the west. Perhaps the Poles might yet see reason, he said hopefully. Perhaps the two countries could reach a peaceful solution after all, if they negotiated together step-by-step. After the first of those steps, the British might abandon the Poles, just as they had the Czechs the year before. Such a suggestion was a far cry from what Ribbentrop had been urging.

Weizsäcker advised Hitler not to hesitate in seizing any opportunity that might present itself—to take advantage of any opening that might lead to more talks with the Poles. But, the baron added, if all that failed and war broke out, there would be nothing more for him personally to do at the foreign office. Should war come, he told Hitler, he wanted to be released and allowed to return to the navy. On that note, Weizsäcker departed, leaving Hitler mulling over what might happen over the next two days. Little time was left. The following day, he needed to send out his written invasion order to the armed forces, and on the day after, Saturday, his soldiers would march into Poland.[1]

He had to be at the center of all this. They needed to go to Berlin immediately, Hitler concluded, ordering his aides to pack. As always, Hitler had acted spontaneously, deciding at the last moment to make his travel plans, and there was much scurrying about as the Nazi brass and their staff rushed to collect papers and clothes for the return flight.[2] Hitler had a radio message dispatched to Ribbentrop's airplane, instructing the pilot to change course to Berlin rather than return to Berchtesgaden. Hitler would hear Ribbentrop's report there.[3]

Outside the Berghof, boots echoed on the stone, and the servants carried out Hitler's luggage while the führer ate his lunch. By three o'clock, he was ready, and an aide helped him into a tan overcoat. Hitler, who was clad in his brown Nazi Party uniform, put on his brown military hat, pulled on a pair of black leather gloves, and walked out and down the stone steps to his waiting Mercedes convertible, one of a fleet of long Mercedes convertibles and limousines. As he descended, he was offered one final view of his mountain world. He was putting behind him this space of freedom in exchange for Berlin's confining buildings.

Hitler climbed into the front passenger seat while his chief military aide, Colonel Rudolf Schmundt, and his valet, Heinz Linge, took seats in the back. Linge sat directly behind the führer so he could provide Hitler with anything he might want. Erich Kempka, his chauffeur, started the car slowly down the drive as the SS guards saluted and lowered from a flagpole on the lawn Hitler's personal standard, a square red flag with a swastika in the center and a gold eagle on each corner. Just behind the Mercedes was an open car filled with SS bodyguards, and trailing it was a procession of other cars that carried Hitler's entourage of aides and ministry officials.[4]

The procession rolled down the winding mountain roads to the airport outside Salzburg. Waiting was a silver trimotor Junkers 52 airplane. Four other J-52s sat beside it to carry the entourage. The Junkers was Germany's standard airliner, the workhorse of Lufthansa. The lead plane, with *D-2600* printed large on its side, had been Hitler's until he acquired a larger, faster four-engine Condor, which could climb nearly a mile higher and fly 240 miles an hour—an impressive speed in 1939. He had provided that plane to Ribbentrop for his trip to impress the Russians and today would use his old aircraft.[5]

The noise from the motors was deafening and much too loud for conversation, so as they flew up over Bavaria and headed north, Hitler sat silent, wondering how the British were reacting to his meeting with Henderson and how to turn around the Italians.

* * *

Four or five hours earlier, Dahlerus had arrived in Berlin and taken a car to the Esplanade Hotel, which was on the Potsdamer Platz, around the corner from Hitler's New Reich Chancellery. There, he learned that he would be picked up at twelve thirty and driven to Göring's estate, Carinhall, where he and the reichsmarschall would meet.

Having heard Göring's warnings that Ribbentrop wanted to kill him, Dahlerus was wary and asked a Swedish friend, a banker who worked in Berlin, to meet with him. The banker, a man named Allan Wettermark, was familiar with the intrigues that went on among the Nazis and warned that Dahlerus could be arrested if he was discussing peace plans with Göring without Hitler's approval. Since Dahlerus had no idea whether Hitler had approved, the two agreed that Wettermark would witness Dahlerus's departure for Carinhall in case the man did not return by nightfall. If that happened, the banker would notify the Swedish counsel.

When they met at two in the afternoon, Göring pointed out that the Russian pact had strengthened Germany's position since it no longer faced a war on two fronts. Resolving the crisis depended largely on Britain, he indicated, and he asked Dahlerus to go to London the next day to let the British know that Germany wanted to reach an understanding and would be happy to discuss it with some senior emissary. Göring also said to tell them that he personally would use all his influence to make that happen. He said he was asking this because he did not believe the foreign ministry able or willing to have relations with the British that were close enough to bring about a peaceful end to the crisis.

Göring announced that he had to go to Berlin at four o'clock for a meeting with Polish ambassador Józef Lipski. After that, he needed to meet with Hitler and Ribbentrop, both of whom were flying in that afternoon.

Göring wanted to continue offering Dahlerus all his thoughts about solving the crisis, so he had someone bring out a two-seat convertible, and he drove the Swede back to Berlin. Göring might not have been popular with men like Ribbentrop, but his record as a war hero and his jovial personality had made him highly popular with the German people. As they moved into the city's traffic, people recognized the reichsmarschall, and when the car stopped for red lights, pedestrians cheered him.

Along the way, Göring said that Neville Chamberlain was to address the House of Commons that afternoon and that he would call later and let Dahlerus know what impression it had made on the German leadership.[6]

* * *

An hour and a half later, Hitler's Junkers touched down at Berlin's Tempelhof field. Hitler stepped out of the aircraft. The temperature was eighty degrees, much warmer than the mountain cool of Berchtesgaden.[7] His long overcoat, wool uniform, and leather gloves were not made for this kind of weather.

He pulled the glove off his right hand, clutching it in his left fist, and raised his arm straight up to acknowledge the salutes of the crowd.[8] The people there had not expected Hitler. They had come to welcome Ribben-trop back from his triumph in Moscow, and among them were a number of diplomats. Hitler spotted Italian ambassador Bernardo Attolico and walked over, smiling, his hand outstretched, trying to charm the man. As they exchanged pleasantries, Hitler's eyes seemed to sparkle in the afternoon sun.

Hitler left for town in another open-topped Mercedes, followed by the usual carload of bodyguards. But this time, a third car followed. It was filled with Berlin policemen. North, into the city, they went, over Kreuzberg, the highest point in town, and on to Blücher Platz and the ornamental 110-foot-wide bridge beyond that spanned the Landwehr Canal, which connected the two ends of the Spree River. In the Belle Alliance Platz, his car roared around the base of the six-story Column of Peace, which Prussians had erected a century before to honor the peace that had come at the close of the Napoleonic Wars.

Usually when Hitler's motorcade roared through Berlin or along the autobahn from the Berghof to the airport, crowds would cheer him. This day, in both places, the crowds were strangely silent.[9]

Berlin was a charming city, but to Hitler, this was by no means an impressive route for a foreign leader to enter Germany's capital. To him, it was a crowded provincial city with many small buildings. There was no broad grand avenue to awe a visitor. He, the great devotee of architecture, had been working with his architect, Albert Speer, making ambitious plans for the city. Once he finished restoring Germany to its rightful place, he would transform this jumble into a new Rome. There would be wide boulevards lined with monuments of granite that would last ten times the thousand-year life of his Third Reich.[10]

Soon, they were turning onto the Wilhelmstrasse, the most famous street in Germany. They passed the new air ministry on their left, a two-thousand-room palace that Göring had built. On the right stood Goebbels's propaganda ministry. Up the street on the left was the Reich Chancellery, since Otto von Bismarck the official residence of Germany's heads of state. The Congress of Berlin had convened there in 1878.

The big black convertible wheeled left into a vast courtyard that was the Court of Honor, the new ceremonial entrance of the New Reich Chancellery, which had been completed eight months earlier and was a wing of the older building. It alone was a mammoth structure, stretching back a block along a side street, a showplace designed to impress visitors with its majesty and opulence. Hitler walked up the broad steps past two saluting SS guards, stepped inside, turned right, entered the Old Chancellery, and went into his two-story apartment, which looked out on a block-long private garden that lay behind the building.

Once settled, Hitler received a briefing from Otto Dietrich's press staff. They had no news from Rome but a disappointing report from London. Despite Ribbentrop's assurances, Chamberlain's government still lived. Hitler's tough talk to Henderson had failed.

In fact, Chamberlain's speech to the House that afternoon had seemed less compromising. Most alarming, the prime minister had talked of the unthinkable—Britain going to war. Despite that, Hitler continued hoping that his meeting with Henderson would yet topple Chamberlain's government. But he could only wait and wonder.

While they were talking, Hitler could hear waves of German bombers rumbling overhead, almost without stop. The Luftwaffe had been sending planes over the city since early morning, practicing for the invasion and, hopefully, reminding the British and French embassies how powerful Hitler's military machine had become. On his ride from Tempelhof, Hitler also had passed workmen installing antiaircraft guns on the roofs of factories, hotels, and office buildings, another signal to the British.

Around seven in the evening, Ribbentrop's car rolled into the chancellery's Court of Honor. Hitler had changed his attire to greet the foreign minister. He now wore black trousers and a double-breasted brown jacket. He, along with Göring, in his formal reichsmarschall's jacket of white, and Ribbentrop, who had on a dark business suit, posed for official photos in front of a curtain printed with roses. Göring's rows of sparkling medals eclipsed Hitler's lone Iron Cross. While Hitler pumped the foreign minister's hand, he told him he was "a second Bismarck." That led Göring to grumble to someone that Ribbentrop should have spent as much time as he had with the Russians trying to win over the British. Ribbentrop looked like an exhausted businessman home from a trip, as he probably had when selling champagne. Hitler had the air of a victorious politician.

As he posed and smiled at Ribbentrop in triumph, Hitler hoped that the photos would have an impact on the British.

Heinrich Hoffmann, Hitler's official photographer, had arrived fresh from his lab with photos he had made of Stalin. Hitler had dispatched Hoffmann on the mission despite protests from Ribbentrop, who had argued that the two airplanes were full. Leave someone behind, Hitler had said. Ribbentrop hated the photographer because Hoffmann was one of Hitler's oldest and closest friends. In fact, Hitler had met his mistress, Eva Braun, through Hoffmann. She had worked in his Munich shop.

Hitler had told Hoffmann he wanted him to go to Moscow because he had two tasks for him. Besides having Ribbentrop meet with Josef Stalin as the German representative, Hitler would break protocol and also send Hoffmann as his personal representative under the guise of delivering a personal message from the führer. His real task was to notice every little thing about the man and, when he returned, provide what amounted to an intelligence assessment of the Russian leader. "An objective and unbiased impression of Stalin and his entourage," Hitler had instructed. "I am interested in trivialities, which often go unnoticed but which often give a much clearer clue to a man's character than all the reports of some silly fathead in the foreign office. So in Moscow, keep your eyes open."

Hoffmann reported that he had found Stalin to be a natural leader, smart and shrewd. He told Hitler he was especially impressed because Stalin could control the entire gathering of subordinates with a mere nod.

Hitler teased the photographer about his enthusiasm for the Russian. "And what have you done with your Communist Party badge?" Hitler asked and grinned.

"It's not there—yet. But you never know," Hoffmann said.

Hitler, Göring, and Ribbentrop, joined by Weizsäcker, had dinner while Ribbentrop told Hitler about his trip. It had been unbelievable, he said. Men whom they had castigated for nearly twenty years had turned out to be fairly civilized. Ribbentrop, wallowing in vanity, went on in detail about the things the Russians had done to flatter him—how he was met at the airport with a guard of honor, how he had been escorted to a small door at the base of the Kremlin wall and had climbed the stairs to a long room. He had expected to find only Molotov there, but Josef Stalin, who had never made himself available to any foreign emissary before, was also waiting for him.

Hitler listened but without any interest. He wanted to know about the treaty. But Ribbentrop kept describing how swept up he had been, at one point declaring he had felt as if he might have been among "old party comrades."

He and the Russians had negotiated through the evening, he said, and by midnight, they had agreed on the terms of the pact and, more important to Hitler, the secret protocol. Now, at last, he was getting to what Hitler wanted to know. The protocol, Ribbentrop went on, would split Poland in two. Russia's sphere of influence would include Rumania, which had a

Fig. 7.1. *From left*, Joachim von Ribbentrop, Josef Stalin, and Vyacheslav Molotov at the signing of the agreement that shocked the world.

defense pact with Britain and could have taken sides against Germany or interfered with Italy's ambitions in the Balkans, where that spring Mussolini had conquered Albania. Moreover, Ribbentrop reported, Germany and Russia could change Poland's borders merely by reaching what was called "a friendly understanding."

This was what Hitler had been waiting to hear. Not only did the treaty allow him to invade Poland, but it enabled him, with Stalin, to carve up the little country and control all of eastern Europe as he pleased.

When Ribbentrop finished, Hitler told him of his speech to Germany's military leaders and that he had ordered the army to prepare to invade on Saturday, now two days away. But, he added, if he were to contain the conflict to only Poland, he needed to ensure that Britain and France stayed out.

He had followed his advice, Hitler told Ribbentrop. When Henderson had visited on Wednesday, he had brought a warning from Chamberlain, but Hitler had made it quite plain he would not budge. Hitler explained that the English had to be kept out of the war either by intimidation or by being bought off—or by both means. He was trying to find a way to persuade the British to back off their support of Poland, and Göring, he said, was setting up an unofficial contact with the English government through his friend Dahlerus.

On that, Göring spoke up, telling them he had met with both Dahlerus and Lipski earlier that afternoon in hopes of setting up two avenues for splitting the Poles from the British. He added that he had dropped the Polish ambassador a hint that Germany's real complaint with Poland was about not Danzig but the country's close ties to Britain.

In his session with Dahlerus, Göring said, he had given the Swede the same message he and Hitler had worked out two days earlier. That, he explained to Ribbentrop and Weizsäcker, included a suggestion that some high-ranking British official come to Berlin and meet privately with Hitler. Perhaps that could win them a second Munich. In fact, he added, he had tried to have Dahlerus call London and ask whether Chamberlain's speech to the House had put Britain on record against holding any talks such as the ones the Swede was to seek.

That news fired Ribbentrop's jealousy once again. His precious domain had been invaded. The führer had listened to Göring and was concerned again about the British.

While Ribbentrop sat there fuming, Hitler and his reichsmarschall agreed that Göring should call Dahlerus immediately and tell him the situation was critical and that England and Germany must move quickly toward an understanding, because the Poles were becoming unmanageable.

Göring went off to call the Swede. It was a quarter past eleven. He reached Dahlerus at the Esplanade Hotel and told him that Chamberlain's speech had been received favorably. But matters were getting out of hand, he said. Dahlerus needed to go to London as soon as he could and inform Chamberlain's government that it was crucial that they begin negotiations immediately.

As Göring was leaving the room, Hitler informed Ribbentrop that they faced another matter of even greater importance than separating the British from the Poles. Only a day remained before the invasion, and unless Germany could present the west with a show of overwhelming force, the British government might well rally. This meant it was imperative that Germany persuade Italy to join in the war with Poland, but, he informed Ribbentrop, the alliance with Italy had come under strain. If Italy refused to stand firmly with Germany in this crisis, Hitler said, he might not be able to show enough strength to intimidate the western powers.

If they wanted to keep Italy with them, Hitler said, they had to send Mussolini a note, bringing him up to date on the terms of the Russian agreement and selling him on the advantages it could bring. He ordered further that Ribbentrop smooth the Italians' ruffled feathers. In the meantime, Ribbentrop was to prime the Italians for the imminent showdown with Poland and Britain.

He needed to move at once, Hitler ordered, and call Ciano that very night, telling him the Polish crisis had become extremely serious. Hitler urged him not to give them the opportunity to back out.

By this time, Göring had slipped back into the room. Dahlerus, he reported, had heard from London that the British still were willing to talk. That news gave Hitler more false hope that Chamberlain's government was indeed in a crisis. But he would not know that for certain until the morning's press briefing.

The meeting then broke up. It was after midnight. As Ribbentrop headed out, Hitler told him again to call Ciano and report back first thing in the morning. Any possible problems with the Italians had to be resolved quickly, for only a little more than twenty-four hours remained before the army would be marching into Poland.[11]

8

ET TU, BRUTÉ?

HITLER WOKE FRIDAY MORNING, AUGUST 25, FULL OF confidence. The day would be sunny and warm but not quite so hot as the preceding day.[1] To Hitler, this would be a glorious day. The Wehrmacht was ready to march, and he would keep the Italians with him.

Ribbentrop soon appeared and said that he had called Ciano at one o'clock that morning as ordered and had assured the Italian foreign minister that Britain and France would not get involved if there were a war with Poland. He had emphasized to Ciano that the situation was critical, claiming that Poland was making more provocations. Ciano, who had found Ribbentrop less overbearing than usual, had suggested that the two meet, but Ribbentrop had evaded the suggestion.[2] Hitler's optimism rose yet higher. Somehow he assumed Mussolini understood the need for using force, and believing Il Duce needed only reassurances about the pact with Russia, Hitler began dictating a note to him. It was a gentle message, yet there was pressure under its cloak of velvet. Trying to overcome Italy's wariness of Russia, Hitler gave his Axis partner a summary of the negotiations that had led to the treaty with the Soviets. Germany could not avoid such a pact, he said, because of the general state of world affairs, meaning the reluctance of the Japanese to commit themselves against Britain and the steady deterioration of Germany's relations with Poland.

"These reasons led me to hasten the conclusion of the German-Russian conversations," he dictated. "I have not yet informed you in detail, Duce, since I had no idea of the possible extent of these conversations, or any assurance of the possibility of their success."

The treaty with the Soviets, he announced, was no less than Poland's death warrant. "I must tell you, Duce," he said, "that, through the agreements, the most benevolent attitude by Russia in case of any conflict is assured."

Then he added, "I believe I may say to you, Duce, that through the negotiations with Soviet Russia a completely new situation in world politics has been produced which must be regarded as the greatest possible gain for the Axis."

He followed those words with his play for Italy's support. He maintained that the Poles were being irresponsible, even running amuck. He painted a picture of an uncontrolled crisis that was trying German patience and leading to an unpredictable, but inevitable, blowup. "In these circumstances no one can say what the next hour may bring," he warned. "I can only assure you that there is a definite limit beyond which I can in no circumstances retreat."[3]

He concluded the note by playing to Mussolini's conscience, saying that as he opened hostilities against Poland, he was counting on "Italy's understanding." Those two words would have unexpected consequences in Rome. "I can assure you, Duce, that in a similar situation I should have complete understanding for Italy and that in any such case you could be sure of my attitude from the outset."[4]

The note dictated, the final draft corrected, Hitler scrawled his signature to it, and Ribbentrop hurried off to telephone the text to Ambassador Mackensen in Rome. The arguments and the tone that Hitler and Ribbentrop had used with the Italians seemed most effective. Many of his points he had made to the military leaders three days earlier, and somehow Hitler thought that pitch had gone down well. Now, God willing, this note would win over the Italian government.

Ribbentrop instructed Mackensen to deliver the note posthaste. It was urgent that Hitler have an equally speedy response from Mussolini, because he was hesitant to sign the final invasion order until he was certain Italy would align itself with Germany.

Soon after, Weizsäcker told Ribbentrop that the Italians would leave the Germans hanging—and immediately.

"I disagree with you one hundred percent. Mussolini is far too great a man to do that!" Ribbentrop shouted.

Weizsäcker also called the Italian ambassador and urged him to talk to his boss in Rome. But Attolico said Ciano was with Mussolini, spending the day on the beach. Actually, they were not on any beach. The two were holed up in Mussolini's office in Rome's Palazzo Venezia, where Il Duce was wavering.

Although Hitler knew nothing of it, Mussolini had been bouncing back and forth for days, between going to war beside Germany and bending to the urgings of Ciano, remaining neutral. Like Ciano, most of Italy—including King Victor Emmanuel—wanted no war, and many disliked the Germans. When Mussolini and his foreign minister had talked of backing away from their promise to fight alongside Germany, Il Duce had been reluctant, fearing the Nazis would take revenge against Italy. The day before, August 24, Ciano had persuaded him to take the path of peace but was finding on the morning of August 25 that Mussolini was all for war again.

As Hitler had been drafting his note to Rome, Ciano—arguing that the king wanted peace—was winning over Mussolini, persuading him to tell Hitler that Italy would stay out of the conflict. Ciano had returned to the foreign ministry with Mussolini's agreement, but before that message could be sent to the embassy in Berlin, Mussolini had summoned Ciano back, telling him that he still feared Hitler's reaction and wanted to join Germany against Poland at once. Ciano had returned to the foreign office, where his staff was astounded at Il Duce's reversal.[5]

* * *

Still convinced he could bring down Chamberlain, Hitler believed more firmly than ever that his performance with Henderson at the Berghof had been worthy of a theatrical prize. The afternoon before, the British House of Commons should have met, and Chamberlain's government should have tumbled into a dusty heap. And with it, the French regime should have gone as well, leaving both his opponents wallowing in seas of disarray.

Fired with expectation, Hitler was eager to see the newspaper and wire service coverage from London, and he summoned Otto Dietrich. The führer explained that he wanted the stories on the British cabinet crisis. Puzzled, Dietrich asked what he was talking about. "The resignation of the British and French governments, of course," Hitler said impatiently. Instead, Dietrich showed him a copy of a statement Chamberlain had delivered to the House of Commons.[6]

The prime minister had begun by telling the House that he had summoned the members from their vacations to take whatever "new and drastic steps" were needed to stand up to Hitler. "The international position has steadily deteriorated until today we find ourselves confronted with the imminent peril of war," he said. Chamberlain also made it quite plain that Hitler had swept away any sympathy the British government might have had for the return of Danzig. Chamberlain was no orator. His style was turgid, his sentences convoluted, but he did make it quite clear that Britain would carry out its pledge to Poland and not bend to Hitler.[7]

More ominous, Dietrich reported, instead of being greeted by the usual catcalls and opposition, Chamberlain's declaration had generated a standing ovation. Moreover, Parliament had passed an emergency powers act, giving the British government dictatorial power and suspending some civil liberties, a most unusual step for a people so known for their love of freedom. Furthermore, he reported, the Royal Navy was said to have strung a barrier across the Skagerrak, the strait that enabled Germany's naval vessels to move from the Baltic Sea to the North Sea.[8]

Hitler was stunned. He could not believe it. Convinced Dietrich was wrong, he summoned his interpreter, Paul Schmidt, from the foreign office next door. Balding and nondescript in appearance, Schmidt was a keen observer of the events unfolding around him. Hitler ordered him to translate for him the exact text of Chamberlain's speech.

Schmidt's translations reaffirmed what Dietrich had read to Hitler. Two sentences in Chamberlain's speech about Germany's pact with Russia hit especially hard. "In Berlin," Chamberlain had said, "the announcement has been hailed with extraordinary cynicism as a great diplomatic victory which removed any danger of war since France and ourselves would no longer be likely to fulfill our obligations to Poland. We felt it our first duty to remove any such dangerous illusion."[9]

Schmidt also translated the speech Lord Halifax, Chamberlain's foreign minister, had delivered to the House of Lords. Until that spring, Halifax had urged Chamberlain to appease Hitler and avoid any major confrontation, but when Germany marched into the Sudetenland, he had swung around, becoming a strong voice against Hitler and pledging that they go to war to protect Poland. Halifax's declaration to the House of Lords repeated Chamberlain's speech to the Commons almost word for word.

The German embassy in London also had wired by radio that the Commons had approved Chamberlain's main points unanimously. The leaders of both the Labour and Liberal Parties were united in their approval. The morning papers, the embassy said, were united as well, both the Conservatives and the left-wingers.

Having finished his translation, Schmidt quietly walked out, leaving Hitler sitting silent, shaken and utterly despondent.[10]

The British are a most resolute race. Julius Caesar had great difficulty conquering their Celtic ancestors. The Romans even had to build a wall to keep the Scots from invading. British blood is infused with that of Norman warriors. The English overthrew one tyrannical monarch, Charles I, and their kin in the colonies successfully resisted George III. The British people did not succumb to threats or intimidation. And they followed a moral principal that led them to fulfill commitments such as their promise to Poland. Hitler did not understand that or the concept of morality in government. He had no inkling of what composed a typical Brit. Ribbentrop had led him to this through his own crass arrogance and woeful ignorance. Now, to his bewilderment, Hitler was confronting all those strengths.

Ribbentrop assured him again that regardless of their words, the British would never support the Poles. Nevertheless, Hitler was unnerved. Henderson might have talked of war in private, but Chamberlain now was making the threat in public—and receiving cheers for it. Hitler now needed the Italians more than ever.

As Hitler's noon deadline to sign the marching orders neared, he summoned General Keitel. Hitler could do nothing until he had Mussolini's support. And the news from London was another roadblock. Embarrassed, he was forced to inform Keitel he could not yet sign the orders. Hitler explained that he had written Mussolini and was awaiting a reply that would confirm the Italians' commitment to join the German invasion. Naturally, he said, the "professionals" in the foreign office would leak the news of Italy's support to the English, and they and the French would be awed into accepting the defeat of Poland without going to war. What, he asked, would be the final hour his generals needed for his order? Keitel said he would find out, and he went off to call his office.[11]

Ribbentrop returned, reporting that the note to Mussolini was at the embassy in Rome. Still shocked at the news from the British press, Hitler said he had expected his letter to Chamberlain to bring down the government. Instead, the British leadership seemed to have united.

Sensing Hitler's uncertainty, Ribbentrop told him his letter had ruled out virtually all further diplomatic moves. Then, backing away from his advice to be tough, he suggested that Hitler make one further try at using negotiations to win over Britain. Hitler thought about it for a few minutes and agreed that they needed some sort of new maneuver. They must have Henderson visit again. Perhaps with a more conciliatory session, using the tones Ribbentrop had employed to win over the Russians, they still could lure the British away from the Poles.[12] Hitler directed him to tell Henderson to appear at one thirty—not much notice, only forty-five minutes away.[13]

Now Keitel was back. If they were to get all their troops into position by jump-off time the next morning, the army leaders had told Keitel's staff, they needed to receive their final orders no later than three in the afternoon.[14] Hitler said they should expect his final word at that hour. With that, he ventured out of his apartment and headed for his office in the New Reich Chancellery.

He had directed the design of the New Chancellery, personally insuring it had all the majesty and theatrical trappings that would make every visitor feel it was a masterpiece of architectural showmanship, the palace of a powerful potentate. It had been built in less than a year by forty-five hundred workmen.

Coming out of the hall that led from the Old Chancellery, Hitler and his retinue strode across the Hall of Honor and through the mosaic room, a hall with walls of red marble and a marble floor that reflected as if it were a mirror. At last, they passed along the Long Hall. It was 480 feet long, twice the length of the Hall of Mirrors at Versailles. It, too, gleamed with marble. At its far end was the doorway to the huge chamber where Hitler received official visitors, awing them with the room's giant crystal chandeliers, its marble floors and columns. Along one side of the Long Hall was a seemingly limitless line of tall windows. Spaced along the opposite wall were five colossal doorways, each crowned with a gigantic mantel of marble. The dark marble of the doorways contrasted with the light marble of the walls around them. On either side of the third doorway, halfway down the hall, stood two SS guards. On each man's sleeve, Adolf Hitler's signature was woven on a silver stripe. Over the doorway, a bronze plaque bore the initials *AH*. Inside was Hitler's private office.

Hitler walked in. The room was in keeping with the grandeur of the hall outside, ninety feet long and forty-five feet wide. Despite its immense size, it was officially one of Hitler's studies, rather than an office. The portal through which Hitler had entered was twice the height of normal doors and topped with the Nazi symbol, a bronze eagle clutching a swastika. On the far side of the room, five windows looked out onto the chancellery garden. Each window was approximately fifty feet tall.

To Hitler's left, near one of the windows, stood his desk, a large ornate piece of furniture. Three chairs faced it, and behind it sat the führer's high-backed armchair of light red leather. A fireplace made of great marble blocks dominated the far end of the room, and in front of it sat a semicircle of easy chairs and a sofa. Above the fireplace hung a portrait of Otto von Bismarck.[15]

Hitler sat by the fireplace with Ribbentrop and Paul Schmidt and waited impatiently. He had decided to be friendly but with a few strong outbursts make Henderson believe the British were pushing him.

Finally, Henderson was ushered in, and Hitler motioned for him to take a seat at the end of the sofa. As he always did when receiving a guest, Hitler sat in a chair next to the sofa's end, his back to the windows. Ribbentrop and Schmidt took chairs as well, and the führer turned to the ambassador and began talking, trying to speak with warmth and an air of sincerity. At their last meeting, he reminded Henderson, the ambassador had said he hoped they still could reach an understanding. He had thought about this, Hitler claimed, and he wanted to create good relations with Great Britain just as he had with the Soviet Union. His conscience, he said, stirred him to make this final attempt to bring them together.

Poland's provocations were becoming intolerable, he said. Then, his voice rising, he listed a litany of complaints about acts he claimed the Poles had committed. They had even fired on civilian airliners, he charged, adding that Ribbentrop's own airplane had been forced to skirt Polish airspace and fly over the Baltic Sea to avoid any fire from Polish batteries. The Polish government said it was not responsible for such acts, Hitler added, but that was only proof that the government had lost control over its military commanders. He then told Henderson that the problem of Danzig and the corridor needed to be resolved.

"Your prime minister yesterday made a speech in the House of Commons which does not in the least alter the German attitude," Hitler said. "The only result of that speech can be a bloody and unpredictable war between Germany and England. But this time, Germany will not have to fight on two fronts, for the agreement with Russia is unconditional and represents a long-term alteration in German foreign policy. Russia and Germany will never again take up arms against each other."

Although no one had any way of knowing it then, less than two years later, Germany would invade the Soviet Union.

Hitler went on to offer something totally unexpected—an alliance with Britain. He promised to support the future of the British Empire, which was beginning to feel pressure from nationalists in India and other colonies.

Also, he announced, he would assure the British Empire of Germany's backing "regardless of where such assistance would be necessary."

In return, he said, he had some "limited" demands about Germany's former colonies. Although he did not go into detail, Hitler wanted at least some of those colonies, which Britain held, returned to Germany. Hitler also proposed that Britain retain its alliance with France and Germany keep its pact with Italy.

He also offered to accept a "reasonable" limit on armaments, telling Henderson that, contrary to the beliefs of some in London, he was not interested in invading France or other countries of western Europe.

This, Hitler said, was his final offer. As soon as they resolved the Polish problem, he would approach the British about the colonial agreement. He urged Henderson to deliver the offer personally. "Take an airplane immediately and fly to your government," he added, offering his personal plane for the ambassador to use.

Henderson said that he was quite prepared to consider Hitler's offer but that the führer should understand very clearly that Britain could not possibly go back on its word to Poland. No matter how eager his government was for better relations with Germany, it could only come to an understanding based on a negotiated settlement between Germany and Poland. Hitler's new pact with the Russians did not change Britain's position, Henderson added.

Hitler explained that he could not guarantee a settlement with Poland, because Poland's provocations might force Germany to intervene at any moment to protect Germans living there.

That was not for the two of them to discuss, the ambassador said and suggested Ribbentrop take it up with Józef Lipski, the Polish ambassador.

Hitler said that Lipski had seen Göring but had not been able to offer any new ideas.

Well, Henderson said, Britain could not abandon Poland. In his view, Ribbentrop and Colonel Beck needed to meet somewhere and find a way out of the crisis. That would save all of Europe from war.

Hitler countered that he had invited Beck for such a talk in March but that the colonel had refused.

With that, Ribbentrop broke his silence and confirmed Hitler's claim. Going even further, he said the message from Warsaw had been so abrupt the Polish ambassador had had to water it down. With that statement, Ribbentrop had almost given away the highly guarded secret that Germany was able to intercept and decipher Polish communications.

Rising to show the ambassador out, Hitler added that once they settled the Polish question, he would make no further claims. And once more, he urged Henderson to forward his proposal to London and even to take up his offer of the personal airplane.[16]

Hitler had done a good job. Henderson returned to his embassy frustrated with the Poles. Shortly afterward, he concluded a report to London by quoting British historian H. A. L. Fisher. "Only once in the whole course of their history," Fisher had written in *A History of Europe*, "have the Poles shown any wisdom."[17]

Just then, Henderson received news that wiped out any sympathy he had for Germany. As Hitler had planned, the British already had heard reports of Hitler's speech to his generals three days earlier. Now, Louis Lochner, Berlin bureau chief for the Associated Press, had leaked to a member of Henderson's senior staff notes that one of the officers had taken of the meeting. It further confirmed that Hitler was serious about invading Poland. Although Lochner described his source as "a general," it might well have been Admiral Wilhelm Canaris, who, as chief of the Abwehr, would have had contacts with men such as Lochner.[18]

Although Hitler had thought word of his speech to the military leaders would have convinced the British to back down, this news had only stiffened London's stand against him. Hitler was misjudging his opponent, yet he did not seem to realize that.

The meeting with Henderson had lasted an hour. In only thirty minutes, Hitler needed to sign the invasion order, yet they were still awaiting a reply from Rome. Apparently, it had taken longer than they realized for the foreign office to translate the letter, for it had not been delivered to Ciano until 2:00 p.m. and was not to reach Mussolini until 3:20 p.m., almost an hour away.[19]

His anxiety growing, Ribbentrop had summoned Attolico to the chancellery in hopes that he had received some word, but when the ambassador came in, he told Hitler he had heard nothing. Hiding his disappointment, Hitler ordered Ribbentrop to take Attolico into another room, call Ciano himself, and get an answer. They were back in only a couple of minutes, with Ribbentrop saying they had not been able to reach him.

While Hitler brooded over Ciano's silence, Ribbentrop gave Attolico what by now had become their standard sales pitch for wooing the Italians, a glowing report of his trip to Moscow. He went on about how the two nations would cease fearing one another; how they would cooperate in world affairs; how Stalin respected the Italians, as well as the Germans; and even how they had included Italy in their toasts. Ribbentrop told Attolico the Soviets were sending a new ambassador to Berlin but that he must not tell anyone.

Finally, Hitler broke in, saying that the pact freed Germany from having to protect itself on two sides. In addition, he said, the treaty would help Germany and Italy in the east, pressuring Romania to cooperate despite its alliance with Britain and France. Furthermore, since Germany's new friend, Russia, sat on Turkey's northern border, the Soviets would counter Britain's strong presence in the Middle East and pressure Turkey to remain neutral.

He had just received Henderson, Hitler said, and he had told the ambassador that Danzig and the corridor did not concern the English. Hitler said he had told the ambassador that any act by Germany to resolve the Polish problem was none of Britain's business, adding that he had warned Henderson he would regard any attempt at involvement as an unfriendly act.

Trying to influence the Italian with drama, Hitler turned to Ribbentrop and groused about the sins of the Poles—how now they had killed seven Germans and a Czech. Then Hitler abruptly sent Attolico back to his embassy.[20]

It was passing three o'clock, and Hitler could no longer delay signing the order to invade. He kept thinking that Mussolini surely would join in fully with Germany. When Mussolini had invaded Ethiopia, Hitler had sided with Italy, thus, despite Rome's silence, Hitler hung on to the belief he would have Italy's support. So Hitler summoned Keitel, who had been waiting in the Long Hall, and at precisely 3:02 p.m., he signed the invasion order and went off to the Old Chancellery for lunch.[21]

Despondent, Weizsäcker saw the order as the start of a world war. "This afternoon has been the most depressing one of my life," the baron wrote in a note for his personal file. "It is an appalling idea that my name should be associated with this event, to say nothing of the unforeseeable results for the existence of Germany and my own family."[22]

In an hour, Hitler was back. He had told Schmidt to extract the major points of his talk with Henderson and transform them into the note verbale. When he arrived in his office, the note was waiting, and Hitler summoned Ribbentrop. He ordered him to have Schmidt take the note directly to Henderson, along with a personal message from the führer. The führer explained that he wished to convey he had always wanted an agreement with the British. It would be a personal plea for Henderson to urge his government to consider Hitler's offer with utmost seriousness. Ribbentrop dispatched Schmidt to the British embassy, just a few doors up the Wilhelmstrasse.[23]

The führer's anxiety over Italy mounted as he paced back and forth across his office, feeling the heat in his woolen party uniform as he awaited Mussolini's reply. His armies were marching already. There, inside the New Chancellery, he could hear the trucks growling through the streets of Berlin.

Despite their concerns about the British and the Italians, Hitler and Ribbentrop had not forgotten the French, and Robert Coulondre, the ambassador from Paris, was scheduled to visit at five o'clock. Back from his errand to the British embassy, Schmidt sat, waiting with Hitler for the Frenchman's arrival.

Suddenly, one of Otto Dietrich's aides interrupted them, handing the führer a news bulletin from London. Reaching for his spectacles, Hitler began reading. Schmidt came around and, looking over the führer's shoulder, read it as well. It was not good news. The British government, the dispatch said, had just announced that it and Poland had signed the mutual aid pact they had agreed to in April, making their alliance official. Hitler sat stunned, saying nothing, hoping it was false.

In minutes, Coulondre was shown in. The ambassador, a man with a dark southern-European complexion, who, as always, was elegantly dressed, took his seat where the British ambassador had been three hours earlier. In hopes of pulling the French away from the British, Hitler began repeating his spiel about the sins of the Poles, his voice rising as he spoke. They might force him into attacking them, Hitler said, adding that even the threat of war with Britain and France would not deter him from rising to the defense of Germany's interest. As he finished railing against the Poles, his voice eased. More softly, he told Coulondre how much he would regret it if all this pushed France and Germany into war with each other. While trying to charm the Frenchman, Hitler was preoccupied with the shocking news from London and Mussolini's ominous silence, and his voice sometimes grew expressionless as he repeated by rote what he had said to Henderson.

Hitler urged the ambassador to convey his statement personally to the French premier, Édouard Daladier, and then he abruptly rose to dismiss Coulondre.

But the ambassador was not to be sent away. With immense gravity in his voice, he asked for permission to respond. "In a situation as critical as this, Herr Reich Chancellor," he said, "misunderstandings are the most dangerous things of all. Therefore, to make the matter quite clear, I give you my word of honor as a French officer that the French army will fight on the side of Poland if that country should be attacked." That was not the quiet, relatively nice, diplomatic tone of Henderson. Then, his voice rising, Coulondre said, "But I can give you my word of honor that the French government is prepared to do everything for the maintenance of peace right up to the last and to work for moderation in Warsaw."

That was not what Hitler wanted to hear. "Then why did you give Poland a blank check to act as she pleased?" he snapped. Coulondre opened his mouth to answer, but Hitler jumped up and began attacking Poland once again. "It is painful for me to go to war against France. But the decision does not depend on me," he said pointedly, reaching out to shake the ambassador's hand and ending the meeting.[24]

*   *   *

Despite his measured performance with Coulondre, Hitler was growing increasingly worried about Mussolini's silence—and for good reason. He had drafted his letter to Mussolini around noon. It had been translated and delivered to the embassy in Rome by two o'clock, but it had not been delivered to Mussolini until around a quarter after three. Now it was nearly six o'clock, and Attolico had just arrived outside to deliver Il Duce's response.

*   *   *

After Von Mackensen had handed the note to Mussolini, he had returned to his embassy, leaving Ciano and Il Duce to study it. The two considered its wording "ambiguous." Then Ciano came upon the sentence "I can assure you, Duce, that in a similar situation I should have complete understanding for Italy and that in any such case you could be sure of my attitude from the outset." He used those words to try to persuade Mussolini to tell Hitler Italy was not prepared to go to war.[25]

*   *   *

Attolico had arrived at the Reich Chancellery with Mussolini's note while Hitler and Coulondre were meeting. As the Frenchman left, an aide informed Hitler that Attolico was in the Long Hall. Relieved that here at last was Mussolini's response, Hitler had Attolico shown in straightaway.

The Italian took his seat opposite Hitler and Schmidt and handed Hitler Mussolini's letter. Mussolini had started out assuring the führer that he fully approved of the treaty with the Soviet Union. Furthermore, he wanted to avoid a break with Japan, and indeed, he had heard that the Japanese were now more favorable toward the treaty than they had been originally. The treaty might change Turkey's leanings as a neutral, thereby upsetting all the plans the British and French had made for the Middle East. Furthermore, he said, he fully understood Germany's position in the Polish crisis and how a tense confrontation could not go on forever.

But, Mussolini added, "if Germany attacks Poland and the conflict remains localized, Italy will afford Germany every form of political and economic assistance which is requested of her. If Germany attacks Poland and Poland's allies open a counter attack against Germany, I inform you in advance that it will be opportune for me not to take the initiative in military operations in view of the present state of Italian war preparations, of which we have repeatedly and in good time informed you, Führer, and Herr Von Ribbentrop." Mussolini added a grim explanation, writing, "According to what the responsible heads of the services tell me, the petrol supplies of the Italian Air Force are so low that they would last for only three weeks of fighting."

Mussolini was backing away. Hitler read on: "Our intervention can, nevertheless, take place at once if Germany delivers to us immediately the military supplies and the raw materials to resist the attack which the French and English would predominately direct against us."

At their meetings, the two had talked of what they viewed as an inevitable battle with Britain, but, Mussolini noted, they had foreseen that war for some time after 1942. "And by that time," he said, "I would have been ready on land, on sea, and in the air."

Then Hitler reached the final paragraph. "I consider it my bounden duty as a loyal friend to tell you the whole truth and inform you beforehand about the real situation," Mussolini offered. "Not to do so might have unpleasant consequences for us all. This is my view, and since within a short time I must summon the highest governmental bodies, I beg you to let me know yours."

Hitler sat in a glacier of sheer anger. Coldly, hardly showing the storm he repressed, he dismissed Attolico. Hitler icily said he would send an answer to Mussolini later.

Schmidt escorted the ambassador out, leaving Hitler brooding at his desk. Without warning, Ribbentrop rushed in. He had received the bulletin from London at the foreign office, and thinking it impossible, he had called the German embassy in London, insisting that it was false, but the embassy sent him the text of the treaty. He had just read it, he said, and all of it was true. If they attacked Poland, it would mean war with England. The man who had assured Hitler that Britain would never go to war now announced that Britain would never go back on its signature. This treaty meant war with England, Ribbentrop exclaimed, and Hitler had to halt the invasion. Hitler thought about it briefly. He agreed, he said, and called for his chief adjutant, Rudolf Schmundt.[26]

This, he told Ribbentrop, was the second piece of bad news he had received that day. "The Italians are behaving just as they did in 1914!" Hitler declared to his foreign minister.[27] Attolico, he explained, had just brought him the reply from Mussolini. Il Duce would not go to war alongside them against Poland.

No one could find Schmundt, and Hitler dispatched a junior military aide to fetch General Keitel, who was waiting outside in the Long Hall. With Keitel were several small groups of officers, standing around waiting for whatever was needed of them.

The general hurried in. Mussolini had finally replied, Hitler told him and began reading aloud some of the more crucial sentences. The Italians were holding back. Their support was not coming—certainly not this night, when it was needed. But that was not all, said the führer, now highly agitated, disappointment and shock apparent in his voice. "Ribbentrop has just brought me a telegram from our embassy in London," he told Keitel, describing how the British had signed their treaty with Poland. Otto Dietrich, he added, had received a similar report from London.

Hitler suspected that the Italian foreign office had tipped off the British that Italy was not prepared to go in with Germany. It was all Italy's fault, he told Keitel angrily. "As soon as they saw the news from Rome about Italy's attitude to the Polish dispute, Britain ratified the treaty!" Hitler was right. The Italians leaked information to the British, and Ciano had been secretly floating to them a proposed compromise. Yet rather than reacting to that news, the British had signed solely because they had made a commitment to Poland.[28]

Keitel had Schmundt, who by now had been found, bring in the invasion timetable that would show the planned location of each army. The troops were moving into their jump-off positions close enough to the border so they could march overnight into Poland and attack at four o'clock. If they camped in their designated positions through the next day, they might be spotted by Polish air reconnaissance, so they had to refrain from moving any closer.

"All troop movements are to be stopped at once! I need time to negotiate," Hitler ordered. He wanted Brauchitsch and Halder immediately, he said, and Keitel rushed out into the Long Hall. "The order to advance must be delayed again," he said to an aide, and an order went out to all the armed forces: "D-day postponed. Further orders follow."

"There will be frightful confusion and a good deal of swearing on the frontier roads," a major said out in the hall. "You diplomats are to blame for this," he said to Schmidt, who was the foreign office's chief interpreter. "You should have thought things out beforehand and not sent us off just as everything starts to look different." Schmidt thought it a harsh criticism but one befitting the man who had made all the bad decisions, the major's commander in chief, Germany's great diplomat, Adolf Hitler.[29]

* * *

The waiting officers began speculating among themselves if this was a temporary halt or if the invasion was being put off permanently. A number hoped it meant no invasion. It now was seven thirty, and night had fallen. More than three-quarters of a million men, composing forty-six divisions of tanks, artillery, and infantrymen, were on their way through the dark to the Polish border. They moved under radio silence. Stopping all of them would be quite difficult. In fact, countermanding an order such as this was unheard of to German officers.

Moreover, it showed an unprecedented weakness at the top. All this was causing Hitler to lose face with the army. As one of the generals who had been there said later, "The picture of confusion presented by the Reich Chancellery at that moment was, for a trained staff officer, both repugnant and horrifying."[30]

Canaris and others who wanted to see Hitler gone considered his action a total loss of dignity. Some attributed it to a nervous breakdown. "Now," Canaris declared, "the peace of Europe is saved for fifty years because Hitler has now lost the respect of the generals."[31] "We as soldiers were considerably shaken by leadership of this kind," Von Manstein wrote later. "The decision to go to war is, after all, the gravest that a head of state ever has to make. How could any man reach such a decision and then cancel it within a few hours?"[32]

Many commanders were notably lacking in enthusiasm for the invasion. As one general wrote in his diary, "I have the feeling the army is not looking forward to the offensive with an overflowing heart." That officer was none other than Fedor von Bock, commander of Army Group North, which was to move in from East Prussia across Poland's northern border. The order to halt the advance had come as a shock. "I was thunderstruck," Von Bock wrote later that evening. In fact, he could not believe it and called Halder, who confirmed it. "Everything is moving!" he told Halder. He would do all he could to halt his troops. "But," he added, "I can't guarantee there still won't be exchanges of fire."[33]

On Poland's southern border, where Army Group South was advancing, its commander, Gerd von Rundstedt, was having dinner with his chief of staff, Erich von Manstein, when the news arrived. Both men thought hopefully this meant Hitler was backing away from an invasion. Their staff was able to stop all the army group's units except for one motorized regiment. Finally, they were able to bring the trucks to a halt by sending an officer in a small plane that landed in the darkness on the road ahead of the regiment.[34]

* * *

Back in Hitler's office, Ribbentrop by this time had calmed down and was curious about what the führer would do now. "What about the Polish solution?" he asked.

"We will send that note to the British," Hitler replied, referring to the note verbale that Henderson would fly out with in the morning. "Then, if they respond to it, then we can still see what to do," he said. "There will still be time."[35]

Hitler then put in a call to Göring, who, besides trying to win over the British, had an air force to run. Hitler said he had stopped the invasion, explaining Mussolini's message and the Anglo-Polish treaty.

Göring asked hopefully whether the cancellation would be permanent.

"No," Hitler replied, "I will have to see whether we can eliminate British intervention." He had sent London a note verbale, Hitler explained, and he had tried to persuade Henderson to fly to London with the message in hopes that the ambassador could marshal sympathy for the Germans and persuade Chamberlain to consider a compromise.

The reichsmarschall had 2,315 aircraft of different types, ranging from fighters for home defense to bombers, transport planes, and reconnaissance aircraft, all waiting for the invasion. If the delay were too long, Poland's rainy fall season would hamper them. "Do you think it will be definite within four or five days?" he asked.

He said he had no idea precisely when he could reorder the attack. They still had time to act, he added, telling Göring in effect that Dahlerus's efforts now could be much more important.[36]

As Hitler dictated his reply to Mussolini, he inveighed against the "disloyal" Italians, but the note was far sweeter and gentler than he really felt. Hitler held his fellow dictator in such respect that he once told some of his intimates that Il Duce was one of the Caesars. Hitler therefore sensed correctly that Italy's stand was not Mussolini's fault.

Hitler believed Mussolini's note was a bluff, and he proceeded to call it. He dictated a three-sentence reply, repeating Mussolini's claim that he lacked supplies and asking him to specify what he needed. "I would ask you to inform me what implements of war and raw materials you require and within what time," he dictated, "so that I may be in a position to judge whether and to what extent I can fulfill your demands."[37]

When Ribbentrop got up to leave with the note, Hitler suddenly turned on him. He was furious. All Ribbentrop's talk of Britain never standing up to Germany, his supposed strategy to keep Italy on Germany's side, had been a resounding failure—and in only one afternoon. More important, Hitler's having to countermand his own order and the resulting chaos had made him a fool in the eyes of his generals, diminishing his statue and even undermining what respect some still had. That loss of standing fired up Hitler all the more, and he made it quite plain that Ribbentrop was unwelcome in the Reich Chancellery. Hitler did not want to see the man until further notice. He was banished to the foreign ministry.[38]

Göring seemed to have won the battle for Hitler's ear.

No sooner was Ribbentrop gone than Colonel Schmundt ushered in Keitel, Brauchitsch, and Halder. With them was Colonel Walter Warlimont, the Oberkommando der Wehrmacht's chief operations officer and one of the men who opposed going to war. Like many other German officers that day, Warlimont was hopeful Hitler's order to halt the troops meant there would be no invasion. But as he entered Hitler's office, Schmundt said to him, "Don't start celebrating too soon. It's only a question of a few days' postponement."[39]

The five officers and Hitler proceeded to go over the major questions that worried them. Would the troop movements toward the border alert the Poles and give away their plans? Was it too late to cover up their plan? In any event, what would the enemy do? The six men considered each question, concluding that no matter whether the Poles had fathomed the true intention of the troop movements, Hitler had no choice. He had to take his chances and wait for another day.

Brauchitsch and Halder asked whether perhaps, given the halt, the troops might be demobilized and placed back on a peacetime status. But Hitler refused. He told them he would give permission for that only after he knew for certain that his demands on Poland would be met. Nevertheless, Hitler promised, the troops would be sent back to garrison in early September if they did not invade. He acknowledged that he could not keep them on alert any longer. If he delayed the invasion further, the rain would hamper them. He now wanted to bring about some kind of negotiation with the British. He expected Henderson would be going to London that evening. Hitler said he had given the ambassador a new offer, and in the meantime, the armies would be forced to wait until he could see whether the British would nibble at his bait. The next day, he added, he would have some idea of what the new invasion date would be. On that note, the generals left.[40]

Hitler went to his apartment in the Old Chancellery for dinner. One of his guests was Hermann Göring. Just as the meal was beginning, the foreign office phoned. Henderson had called Weizsäcker to say that he had decided to take Hitler up on his offer and use the airplane to London, where he could discuss Hitler's offer personally with Halifax and Chamberlain. Hitler received the news with growing hope that his message would bring the British around.[41]

As dinner went on, Hitler and Göring talked about the day's events and speculated about the next day. But they were interrupted when Göring was called away for a phone call. It was Birger Dahlerus, from London.

Dahlerus had spent the afternoon with his English business friends and through them had sent a report to 10 Downing Street. Early in the evening, he had gone to the foreign office for a session with Halifax, who, waiting for Henderson's arrival, informed him that oral reports of the ambassador's meeting with Hitler had left him more optimistic. Apparently, Henderson's reaction to Hitler's speech before the military leaders had not affected matters in London. Halifax felt the talks had reopened diplomatic channels between the two countries, and to him, it looked as if they would no longer need Dahlerus's services. The Swede had dinner afterward with his British business friends, all of whom seemed to believe their great diplomatic problem was on the course of a resolution. Despite their optimism, they all agreed that Dahlerus should call Göring to assess the mood in Berlin.

Although all telephone communications had been shut down between Germany and Britain, the British foreign office was able to get his call through. When Göring came to the telephone, he gave Dahlerus the impression he was exceedingly nervous and worried. War might break out at any minute, he said, emphasizing his hope that Dahlerus's trip to London would produce results.

All this fear of war breaking out momentarily was quite a change from the way Göring had sounded on the phone the evening before, Dahlerus said. He asked why that was. Göring played coy and answered vaguely and, finally, bit by bit, let the Swede know that it was because the British had signed the pact with Poland that afternoon. Speaking obtusely, Göring let him know that Hitler saw that as a challenge, evidence Britain was not interested in a peaceful solution to the crisis. He urged Dahlerus to do all he could to arrange a meeting between a high-ranking British representative and the Germans.

Göring hung up, hoping that his performance on the phone and the führer's note to Chamberlain would lead the British to rethink their sense of obligation to the Poles. But the fear he had displayed picking up the phone still haunted him.[42]

9

"IT'S ENOUGH TO KILL A BULL"

I**N ROME THE NEXT MORNING, SATURDAY, AUGUST** 26, Mussolini and Ciano were busy discussing Hitler's demand for a laundry list of the supplies they would need if they joined Germany in the invasion. The night before, as Mackensen and Ciano drove to deliver Hitler's note to Il Duce, the ambassador urged the foreign minister to put on the list everything he could think of. Mackensen was opposed to Ribbentrop's warlike policy and figured they'd craft a list so impossible to fulfill that it would stop Hitler.

Mussolini had ordered Ciano to return at ten in the morning with the leaders of Italy's army, navy, and air force. As they gathered outside Il Duce's office in the Palazzo Venezia, Ciano found that most of them were overly optimistic about their forces' strengths and preparedness. This, he found, was especially true of the army's chief of staff, Alberto Pariani. They needed to tell Mussolini the whole truth about their supplies and not be, as Ciano phrased it, "criminally optimistic." Accordingly, in their meeting, they provided Mussolini with a list of all the supplies they would need. They left nothing out. "It's enough to kill a bull," Ciano noted jubilantly in his diary.[1]

* * *

It was hot in Berlin that Saturday. At one thirty that afternoon, Bernardo Attolico rode from the Italian embassy to the New Reich Chancellery to deliver the list and an accompanying note to Hitler. Attolico, Hitler, and Schmidt met in the semicircle of chairs and sofa that sat before the fireplace in Hitler's study. When the ambassador handed him Mussolini's list, Hitler was stunned. It totaled seventeen million tons of raw materials. Il Duce wanted six million tons of coal, two million of steel, seven million of petroleum, one million of copper, and more. Mussolini said, too, that he needed 150 antiaircraft batteries and the ammunition they required to protect his factories. Italy had already requested crucial machinery from Germany, Mussolini reminded Hitler.

"It is my duty to tell you," Mussolini's letter said, "that unless I am certain of receiving these supplies the sacrifices I should call on the Italian people to make—certain though I am of being obeyed—could well be in vain and could compromise your cause along with my own."

Then, at the letter's end, Il Duce offered to help Hitler find a peaceful solution to the crisis.[2]

Hitler was furious, and as he sat stunned and seething, Keitel came in. Hitler told him to look at the list of materials the Italians said they needed in order to join them, adding that there had to have been a slip of the pen. Perhaps someone had heard incorrectly when the note was telephoned to Berlin. Those tonnages seemed improbably high. Hitler asked Keitel to check again, repeating that someone must have incorrectly recorded the figures.

No, Attolico said quickly, the figures were absolutely correct. Then, trying to do what he could to hold off the conflict, the ambassador added something that was totally false: all the materials the Italians sought had to be delivered before Italy could go to war.

Hitler ordered Keitel to call the German military attaché in Rome and have him see whether the chief of the Italian high command himself thought these were their maximum requirements.

Attolico and Keitel left, and as soon as the ambassador was out the door, Hitler went into another scourging denunciation of the Italians. He and Keitel were already suspicious of the Italian diplomatic corps and the nation's royal faction, all of whom were known to be anti-German. Now they suspected the Italians were inflating their demands to such a level the Germans could never meet them. That way, they both believed, the Italians could get out of their obligation. Yet for all his denunciations against the Italians, he never cast any blame on his Fascist friend Benito Mussolini.[3]

For the next two hours, Hitler conferred with his top generals. Keitel, who had called the embassy in Rome, reported that Germany's military attaché had found the tonnages in the letter to be correct. And, Keitel said, his own experts on the high command conveyed that German industry could meet some but not all of Mussolini's demands.

They all seemed to agree with Hitler that they were being bluffed. Brauchitsch advised against sending anything. This all fit Göring's argument that they stay at peace, and he agreed with the reichsmarschall. This was way too much to send, they said.[4]

Hitler said he would counter the Italians' bluff, but only in part. He would offer to come up with what supplies were available, but he would stipulate that he could not deliver them by invasion day and therefore could not expect Rome's active support.

"Those requirements could be met in full as regards coal and steel," Hitler dictated. "But," he said, "it would be impossible for Germany to deliver seven million tons of petroleum. At the moment I cannot state exactly what amount we could contribute." He went on to list what materials they could send and what were not available. He also offered some of the aircraft batteries the Italians had requested but said he could deliver them only over the next year, not immediately. "Since Attolico described this request for immediate delivery of all the material before the outbreak of war as decisive, I regret that I regard it as impossible to fulfill your requests," he concluded.

But he mentioned there was one other service Mussolini could render. Hoping to wring the minimum from the Italians, Hitler made a request. "I understand your position," he said, "and would only ask you to try to achieve the pinning down of Anglo-French forces by active propaganda and suitable military demonstrations." He then tried to reassure Mussolini. France and Britain could do little in the west right away, and since it had air superiority and Russia now was friendly, the German army could deal with them unencumbered after it had smashed Poland. Therefore, he wrote, "I do not shrink from solving the Eastern question even at the risk of complications in the West."[5]

Schmidt translated the dictation, a secretary typed the note, Hitler signed it, and it was sent over to the foreign ministry, where someone would telephone it to the ambassador in Rome.[6]

Meanwhile, Hitler told his generals that he had not decided what to do about reordering the invasion. Before he could plan further, he needed to see what Mussolini had to say about his request for help. Moreover, Henderson might be back with an answer from London. That, he said, could mean some change in Britain's stand.

Soon after their departure, word came from Italy's Ciano, saying their ambassador had been mistaken when he had told Hitler all the materials must be delivered before war could begin. Hitler dismissed the correction. The Italians were looking for a way out, and they now had it. Besides, Germany could never deliver some of the materials on the list, no matter how much time Mussolini allowed.[7]

A message from London also came in. Henderson would not be returning that evening. In fact, he would not be back until late the next day, Sunday. The British government had sent word that it was considering Hitler's message "with care" and that a reply to Hitler would be considered at a meeting of the full cabinet on Sunday. Henderson planned to return after the meeting, hopefully with a reply.[8]

The shadows were lengthening along the gravel pathways in the garden outside, where Bismarck had once walked. At seven o'clock, Robert Coulondre arrived with a letter from France's president, Édouard Daladier. It was a response to the message Hitler had presented to Coulondre the afternoon before.

The epistle was an eloquent plea to avoid war. A peaceful solution, Daladier had written, would not tarnish the honor of the German nation. All the grievances that Germany had cited against Poland could be assured of a fair settlement if submitted to negotiation, the letter said, and France wanted to live peacefully with Germany. Yet despite its talk of peace, the letter was couched, as well, with a tone of unmistakable firmness. "Unless you attribute to the French people a conception of national honor less high than that which I myself recognize in the German people, you cannot doubt either that France will be true to her solemn promises to other nations such as Poland, which, I am certain, also want to live in peace with Germany."

Hitler read on, and the eloquence rose, until at the very close it became a virtual hymn for peaceful coexistence. "If the blood of France and that of Germany flows again, as it did twenty-five years ago, in a longer and even more murderous war," Hitler read, "each of the two peoples will fight with confidence in its own victory, but the most certain victors will be the forces of destruction and barbarism."[9]

The ambassador proceeded to amplify the letter, trying to motivate Hitler to find a peaceful solution to the crisis. But Hitler seemed undaunted, insisting that the British guarantee had stiffened Poland's back. But Coulondre said that the führer had built an empire for Germany without shedding blood and there was no reason to begin it now.

"It is useless," Hitler replied. "Poland would not give up Danzig, and it is my will that Danzig, as one of the ports of the Reich, should return to Germany."[10]

Daladier had asked that Hitler respond to the note, and the führer assured Coulondre that he would. The ambassador suggested, as well, that they keep secret the contents of both Daladier's letter and Hitler's reply until further notice, and Hitler agreed.[11]

The Frenchman left, and Attolico arrived with Mussolini's response. It was evident that Germany could not possibly come through with what Italy had asked, Il Duce's note read. Therefore, Mussolini said, "I will adopt the attitude which you advise, at least during the initial phase of the conflict, thereby immobilizing the maximum Franco-British forces, as is already happening, while I shall speed up military preparations to the utmost possible extent." Then, for the second time that day, Mussolini concluded the note with an offer to help broker a peaceful settlement.[12]

Meanwhile, expecting written orders to follow, Keitel's staff was working on the assumption that the invasion would be launched the next Thursday or Friday, six or seven days away.[13]

Hitler pondered Mussolini's answer further. He was carrying a piece of paper, apparently Mussolini's note, when he walked into the Old Chancellery's conservatory, where his entourage of friends and followers was gathered for dinner. To Albert Speer, he looked exhausted. "This time, the mistake of 1914 will be avoided. Everything depends on making the other side accept the responsibility," Hitler told them. "In 1914, that was handled clumsily. And now, again, the ideas of the foreign office are simply useless. The best thing is for me to compose the notes myself." With that, his entourage went to dinner without him, and Hitler went to his apartment upstairs to dictate another note to Mussolini.[14]

He needed to muzzle the Italians. The British must never know that Germany was standing up to them alone. He could trust Mussolini to be discreet, but Hitler did not trust the others in Rome—and for good reason. He told Schmidt to write that he respected Il Duce's reasons for failing to back Germany but that the world must not learn of it. Therefore, Hitler dictated, he asked that Mussolini use the media and whatever other means that were available to make the British and French fear that Italy might be on Germany's side. "I would also ask you, Duce, if you possibly can, by demonstrative military measures, at least to compel Britain and France to tie down certain of their forces, or at all events to leave them in uncertainty."[15] If that worked, it could force the French to keep troops along the Italian border and the British navy to remain in the Mediterranean.

To reassure Mussolini that he would be on the winning side, Hitler added that if his invasion did trigger a major war, he would vanquish Poland before France and England could act. If that should happen, he had Schmidt write, he would take on the other two powers "with forces which will be at least equal to those of France and Britain." If the British tried to set up a naval blockade such as the one during the past war that had left Germans in starvation, he added, it would have little impact because food would be available from Russia, thanks to the new treaty. He concluded by asking Mussolini to send him workers to man both Germany's factories and farms.[16]

With that, Hitler stopped his dictation. By the time he scrawled his signature to the final copy, it was close to midnight, and although he was normally up into the early hours of the morning, Hitler decided to turn in early. The great rooms of the Chancellery were darkened, and he retired for the evening. But just as he was going to sleep, an aide knocked on the door to say that Göring was outside and needed to see him. It was urgent.

Göring's Swedish contact, Birger Dahlerus, was back from London, he reported, and he had brought a message from Lord Halifax. It was a short note, and Göring gave Hitler a rough translation. The British government was still studying Hitler's note verbale that Henderson had taken to London the previous day. And, the note said, the British most definitely wanted to come to an understanding with Germany. Fired by new hope, Hitler listened closely to Göring's account of Dahlerus's meetings in London.

Göring reported that Dahlerus had found the British preparing for war when he arrived in London that morning. Some people were moving their families from London to safer parts of the country. Train service had been slow because the railroads were busy with military movements. The government seemed eager to have the Swede meet with Göring, and to expedite his trip, the air ministry had arranged for the airline to hold its departing flight for Amsterdam, where the British had arranged a speedy connection to Berlin.

Dahlerus had told Göring the British did not believe Hitler's claims that the Poles were mistreating Germans. Moreover, Göring said, Dahlerus had confirmed his own warnings that an invasion of Poland would rouse Britain to arms. There was no question Britain would stand behind its pact with Poland. But, he said, there also was no question the entire British government wanted to reach an agreement with Germany, so long as Hitler kept the peace. Göring also told Hitler the letter from Halifax was unofficial but that it was supposed to be a prelude to the message Henderson was to bring back to Berlin.

Upon hearing that the Germans were upset over the signing of the treaty with Poland, a representative from the British foreign office had told

Dahlerus that the signing was merely a matter of form—a normal sequel to the oral agreement they had made in the spring. Dahlerus had told Göring the British did not want the signing to interfere with their negotiations with Germany.

The reichsmarschall then told Hitler that he could talk with Dahlerus himself if Hitler wanted. The Swede was only around the corner at the Esplanade Hotel. Hitler dispatched two adjutants, both colonels, to fetch Dahlerus, whom they found in the hotel's lounge. He had been waiting there in case he might be summoned.

By now, the chancellery again was ablaze with lights. The two colonels escorted Dahlerus to Hitler's study in the New Chancellery, where he, Hitler, and Göring took seats in the usual semicircle beside the fireplace.

With little preamble, Hitler began to speak of his desire to reach an understanding with Britain. Complaining of problems he claimed he had encountered since becoming chancellor, and accusing the British of not helping, he launched into an attack on the British. He went on for about twenty minutes, growing increasingly excited, while Dahlerus grew increasingly impatient. "The whole scene was a typical proof of Hitler's demagogic desire," the Swede later wrote, "and a typical specimen of the method he used to force his point of view upon either adversary or interlocutor."

Dahlerus was beginning to fear that instead of achieving something, the meeting would be nothing but a long monologue by the führer. So when Hitler paused for a second, Dahlerus interrupted, saying he regretted Hitler did not share his opinion of Britain and its people. "I lived as a working man in England for some time, and I know all classes of Englishmen," he said.

Unexpectedly, that caught Hitler's interest. "What's that? You have worked as a common laborer in England?" he asked. "Tell me about it."

Most likely, Dahlerus was the only person Hitler had ever talked to who could tell him about the English working class. Surely Ribbentrop could not. He knew only rich aristocrats who feared the Communists and favored the Reich. And many of Göring's contacts were in the military.

Hitler forgot his diatribe against Britain, and the two went into a long discussion of the British. Hitler would ask questions about them, and Dahlerus would respond, stressing his respect for the English people. He gave several examples of their qualities and endurance and how stubborn they could be when they had a cause.

No matter, Hitler retorted, there were numerous inept plutocrats there.

That, Dahlerus replied, was true not only in England. Such people could be found in every country, Germany included.

They continued talking for at least a half hour. Dahlerus felt more confident as they progressed, recognizing Hitler as a man who lacked any real knowledge of Britain and had formed his impressions solely from the negative reports of his foreign advisers, meaning Ribbentrop. So he told the führer that if he had the opportunity to get to know the British Empire and its people well, and if he gained a better knowledge of the British mentality, there would be some real hope of the two nations getting together.

That set Hitler off into another monologue. He began pacing across the long room, growing more excited by the minute. He described his last meeting with Henderson. Hitler was eloquent and highly persuasive, but to his dismay, Dahlerus could see that the man was unable to understand or even respect any opinion but his own.

Hitler concluded his little speech by declaring that his offer to Henderson would be the last he would make to Britain. The Reich was powerful, he declared, emphasizing Germany's military might and saying it had been his creation. Berlin's antiaircraft batteries alone, he claimed, were as strong as what the entire British Empire had. That brought a chuckle from Göring. A German infantry company was so well trained and well equipped with antitank guns and automatic weapons, Hitler said, his generals could send it on any sort of mission. No chuckle from the reichsmarschall that time. And as Hitler talked on, his face seemed to stiffen, and he began moving his arms in a strange way. Hitler admitted that the British navy was indeed a formidable foe, but he said his U-boats made the German navy superior. He impressed his visitor with his technical knowledge, detailing the thickness of the deck armor in various types of British warships.

Dahlerus said that Germany certainly had staged a highly successful rearmament but that the other major nations had done so as well. Moreover, Britain, protected by its fleet, had the endurance to keep on producing armaments as it had done in World War I, something Germany seemed to forget.

Dahlerus spoke slowly and quietly to avoid irritating the führer, and while Hitler initially listened without interrupting, he suddenly stood, appearing excited and nervous, pacing up and down, talking as if to himself, saying that Germany was invincible and could defeat its enemies in a rapid war. Then, just as suddenly, he stopped walking and stood in the middle of the room, staring, his eyes glassy. Then he resumed speaking in staccato phrases. "If there should be a war," he declared, "then I will build U-boats, build U-boats, U-boats, U-boats, U-boats." Hitler's voice lowered to a mumble so low that his words could not be distinguished. The he pulled himself together and raised his voice as if addressing a huge crowd: "I will build airplanes. Build airplanes, airplanes, airplanes, and I will destroy my enemies!"[17]

Dahlerus sat amazed. He looked at Göring to see his reaction, but the reichsmarschall showed none. To Göring, Hitler might only be putting on another show, as he had before Henderson. But to Dahlerus, he was abnormal—emotionally unhinged. This man, Hitler, was holding the fate of the world in his hands, the decision to go to war or establish peace. *This is the man whom so many have described to me as fascinating*, he thought. He wondered whether Göring had the strength to contend with Ribbentrop's influence and possibly gamble his own position in the hierarchy to lead Hitler away from war.

Hitler talked on. Dahlerus thought he sounded as if he were in a trance. "War doesn't frighten me. Encirclement of Germany is an impossibility. My people admire and follow me faithfully," Hitler said, his eyes wandering. "If the enemy can hold out for several years, I, with my power over the German people, can hold out one year longer. Thereby, I know that I am superior to all the others."

Now he was pacing again. He stepped up in front of the Swede and came to a halt. "Herr Dahlerus, you who know England so well, can you give me any reason for my perpetual failure to come to an agreement with her?"

Hitler was so agitated that the Swede hesitated because he was afraid of Hitler's reaction if he answered too honestly.

Quietly, carefully, Dahlerus said, "Your Excellency, with my comprehensive knowledge of the English people, their mentality, and their attitude towards Germany, I must definitely assure you that I am absolutely convinced that these difficulties are founded on a lack of confidence in you personally and in your government."

Hitler flung out his right arm and hit his chest with his left hand. "Idiots! Have I ever told a lie in my life?" For a politician, that was an astounding claim, especially for one who was breaking the solemn promise he had made at Munich.

Dahlerus said that politics were probably like the business world. No one came to a good agreement without mutual trust. If that were not there, regardless of the reason, it had to be created or restored.

Fig. 9.1. In happier times, Mussolini and Hitler met to discuss the upcoming surrender of France. It was June 1940 when Göring (*far left*) and Hitler greeted Mussolini (*right*) and his son-in-law and foreign minister Galeazzo Ciano (between Hitler and Göring) at Munich's railroad station.

Hitler continued walking back and forth, then stopped and pointed at the Swede. "You, Herr Dahlerus, you have heard my side. You must go to England at once and tell it to the British government. I do not think that Henderson understood me, and I really want to bring about an understanding."

Being a private citizen, Dahlerus said, he could not go to London on Hitler's behalf, but if the British expressed a wish to hear about their conversation, he would be willing to go. If so, he added, he needed a clear picture of what Hitler wanted if he were to reach an agreement with England. For instance, he said, he would need to know what kind of corridor Hitler wanted.

For the only time that evening, Hitler smiled. He turned to Göring. "Well, Henderson never asked about that."[18]

When Dahlerus pointed out that he would need to be armed with absolutely precise information on what land Hitler wanted, Göring picked up a nearby atlas, tore out a page, and outlined in red pencil the territory Hitler had in mind. Hitler then described the points he had given Henderson and added one that he had not before mentioned—a guarantee of Poland's borders.

As they concluded, Hitler emphasized his offer to support Britain if it ever were attacked. Wherever Britain was threatened, he said, Germany would come to the country's assistance. Göring, who had remained silent through most of the session, joined in, asserting that even if Italy should confront Britain, Germany would support the British.

The meeting had gone on until four thirty in the morning. His hopes soaring that Dahlerus might persuade the British to reach an accord, Göring took the Swede outside and had an aide arrange for a German airplane to carry him nonstop to London's Croydon Airport at eight o'clock. Dahlerus returned quickly to his hotel, where he called his British contact, Charles Spencer. London, Spencer said, would be expecting him.[19]

10

THE SPEECH THAT FELL FLAT

HITLER'S OFFER TO SUPPORT THE BRITISH EMPIRE "REGARDLESS of where such assistance would be necessary" could have included the Mediterranean. Göring even defined it that way to Dahlerus. The British had interests at both ends of the Mediterranean, which Italy considered its own. The ancient Romans had named it Nostrum Mare, or Our Sea, and Mussolini viewed it as definitely his. The mere idea of their ally supporting England if the country confronted Italy for control of the Mediterranean would be unthinkable to Mussolini and Ciano.

So on Sunday morning, August 27, seeking to divide the two allies or lead Mussolini to pressure Hitler to avoid war, the British had their ambassador in Rome, Percy Lyham Loraine, give Ciano a copy of Hitler's proposal. Ciano hid his surprise and pretended he already knew of the offer. Inwardly, he was outraged. So was Mussolini, when Ciano told him.

Ciano then telephoned Halifax. Their chat was quite friendly, and the Englishman said Britain would not reject Hitler's offer, although it would stand behind its guarantee to Poland.

Led by his ego rather than common sense, Mussolini believed Hitler was doing this because he feared that Il Duce would steal prestige from der führer by stepping in and settling the crisis through diplomacy. Ciano doubted that. He viewed the Germans as "treacherous and deceitful" people with whom Italy should never have any alliances.[1]

* * *

In Berlin, Ribbentrop, now in his second day of banishment, was making life miserable for all his subordinates. It was never easy living with Ribbentrop, but this situation made it impossible. The foreign ministry had moved only recently into the former presidential palace, which was next door to the Reich Chancellery. Being so close to where everything was happening made the pain all the more severe for Ribbentrop. It grated on him, and he took out his frustration on anyone unfortunate enough to be in his presence.[2]

Twice, Ribbentrop was offered opportunities for keeping the peace. The evening before, Attolico had visited Weizsäcker with a message from Mussolini, offering to mediate. Sunday morning, an intermediary brought an offer from the counselor at the Polish embassy for mediation by the monarchs of Belgium and Holland. Ribbentrop declined both offers, saying Britain was bluffing about war. As soon as any sign of a peaceful solution emerged, Weizsäcker sadly wrote in his diary, "Ribbentrop nipped it in the bud."[3]

That morning, when he heard of Hitler's meeting with Göring and Dahlerus, Ribbentrop grew all the more infuriated. He was so angry that when Attolico called, asking whether there was any news, Ribbentrop told him there was little chance of peace. He said Henderson had gone to London only to express his personal views, not to deliver any messages, which the Italians knew was a flagrant lie. Attolico's boss, Ciano already viewed Ribbentrop as little better than scum, and that statement solidified his opinion. "Can there ever be a more revolting scoundrel than Von Ribbentrop?" he recorded in his diary.[4]

Next door at the Reich Chancellery, Hitler looked haggard when he sat down to breakfast. Since he was used to lying awake until nearly dawn, the late-night meeting with Dahlerus should not have been a great problem, but he had been fatigued already, and now he was paying for his session with Göring and the Swede. In addition, the muggy, oppressive weather was likely making it more difficult for him.[5]

Across the nation, from Hamburg to Munich, there was growing anxiety. No one wanted a repeat of the world war, and crowds of worried Berliners had formed in the Wilhelmstrasse outside the Reich Chancellery. Chauffeurs asked any passenger heading to or from a government office whether war was imminent. Even food was becoming scarce, likely because people had begun hoarding, causing the government to set up rationing.

If the people were concerned, the leaders of the Nazi Party might well be too. The Reichstag members had been waiting in Berlin, many of them in hotels, for a session Hitler had planned to hold the previous day, Saturday, after invading Poland. Some knew of his speech to the generals. Some wondered about the state of his negotiations. So sensing all this, Hitler had ordered that they convene that Sunday afternoon at the chancellery.

First, though, Hitler had to respond to the letter from Daladier that Coulondre had delivered the previous evening. He believed he needed to answer with warmth but also strength. He would give nothing and stand more firmly than ever on his earlier demands. Moreover, no matter what retribution France might threaten, he wanted to emphasize that a showdown was forthcoming. Guided by that, Hitler began to dictate.

He started with what he considered a gentle touch, saying that once Germany had retaken the Rhineland, she had renounced any further claims in the west, including Alsace-Lorraine, the French provinces that Bismarck had seized in the Franco-Prussian War and that the Treaty of Versailles had returned to France. Although Germany had stuck by its commitment to make no further claims in the west, Hitler said, Germany had not renounced any of her claims to eastern lands that the Treaty of Versailles had taken away.

While Hitler was dictating, Keitel came in, and Hitler told him he had no time for him. Daladier had written, Hitler said, calling on him as an old soldier to do everything he could to avoid war. Hitler said that someday Keitel should look at Daladier's letter, for, apart from its humanitarian concerns, it showed how the French were thinking. It clearly illustrated they had no intention of ever going to war over the Polish Corridor, Hitler said.

The general left, and Hitler went back to dictating. He tossed out the same old charge against the British. He had made an offer to the Poles, he said, but Britain, with its defense pact, had encouraged the Poles to refuse to agree. "Polish public opinion, firmly convinced that Britain and France would fight for Poland, began making demands that might, perhaps, be dismissed as ridiculous lunacy if they were not so infinitely dangerous," he said. Then, as usual, he accused the Poles of committing atrocities against German minorities.

How would Daladier act, the letter asked, if a portion of France, such as Marseille, were taken away and the Frenchmen there persecuted? "You are a Frenchman, Monsieur Daladier, so I know how you would act. I am a German, Monsieur Daladier. Do not doubt my sense of honor or my consciousness of my duty to act in just the same way."[6]

Making it plain he was not budging, he dictated on, repeating his demand that Danzig and the corridor be returned to Germany and that the so-called atrocities be stopped. He then began summing up. If they should go to war, Hitler said, there would be a difference in the causes they would be fighting for. "I, Monsieur Daladier, would then be fighting with my people to right an injustice done to us, and the others would be fighting to perpetuate this injustice." Having no idea how concerned the public was about the threat of another war, Hitler thought that, too, would make good copy for the average German. He concluded the letter by warning that he saw no chance of his persuading Poland to show reason.

Satisfied by his creation, Hitler instructed the Luftwaffe to fly the original to Paris for special delivery to the premier himself. He had a copy sent over to the foreign ministry for delivery to Coulondre, with instructions that the ambassador be warned that there had been more incidents along the Polish border and that Germany soon would be forced to retaliate. That message and the letter, he thought, would convince the French to back away. But Hitler understood the French no better than he understood the English.[7]

Now it was time to address the Nazi Party leaders. Five of Hitler's most trusted lieutenants appeared at the door of his apartment to escort him to the meeting. There was thirty-nine-year-old Heinrich Himmler, a Bavarian who had marched in the Beer Hall Putsch and now ran the dreaded Gestapo—or secret police—and headed the SS troopers who guarded Hitler. With him was his protégé, Reinhard Heydrich. Himmler wore glasses with round frames that made him look bookish, concealing the deadly power he wielded, while Heydrich, with his steel-blue eyes, long sharp nose, and blond hair, looked sinister in his black SS officer's uniform and a high-peaked hat with a silver death's head on the crown. Behind them walked another SS officer, Karl Wolff, chief of Himmler's personal staff.

With them hobbled Joseph Goebbels. Although, as propaganda minister, he churned out stories about the Poles' alleged atrocities, Goebbels was still hopeful they would find a way to avoid war. Goebbels's small stature, thin body, and large bony head made him look like an oversize gnome. Like Goebbels, the fifth man in the group, Martin Bormann, wore the brown uniform of the Nazi Party. Bormann, Hitler's private secretary, was little known at the time but would later become a dreaded functionary in Hitler's court. Bormann's square build, bull neck, and heavy head, as well as the scar on his forehead, made him look like a thug and a brawler, precisely what he had been before becoming a Nazi functionary.

Hitler indicated he was ready to go, and the six of them set off through the chancellery's polished corridors. Ahead of them goose-stepped three SS guards. Into the New Chancellery they went, the guards' heels clicking loudly on the marble floor. At the end of the Long Hall, they entered the immense chamber where Hitler held diplomatic receptions. Only about three hundred of the Reichstag's eight hundred delegates were in attendance.[8] As the führer entered, the delegates and party leaders jumped to attention, flinging out their right arms with the Hitler salute. Hitler took his place behind the lectern and faced them with an impassive countenance.[9]

At least some of those in the room noticed that Hitler looked tired and moved more slowly than usual. Fatigue and strain showed in his face and eyes. When he began his speech, his voice croaked, and rather than flowing in a smooth stream as was usual, his words were disjointed.[10]

Hitler was preoccupied. He was worried. Intercepts of the embassy telephones were paying off, but the news had not been good. The conversations reflected a much firmer note than Hitler had hoped for. Taps of the British and French phones revealed that, somehow, they had learned of the postponed invasion, which had prompted discussion of never yielding to Hitler so long as he had troops poised on the Polish border. Also, the British counsel had told Coulondre that Henderson was working to gain time. That was not the tone of someone willing to give in.

There was another piece of disturbing intelligence as well. The Germans had intercepted a call between Coulondre and Daladier. Rather than avoiding war, as Hitler had predicted, the ambassador indicated he was pessimistic about their chances for peace. Should the Germans invade Poland, said one of them, probably Daladier, "I put my confidence in the strength of the [French] nation."[11]

Hitler grew concerned that his letter to Daladier might not have enough impact to counter Coulondre's pessimism. Moreover, he was worried about the response Henderson would bring from London, and he was waiting to hear from Dahlerus as well.

In spite of Hitler's worries, his purpose here was to rouse these men and reassure them. Many knew that the public feared a new war, and others knew the invasion had been postponed and wondered why. Hitler began speaking, saying the situation was grave. But, he added, he was determined to settle the Polish crisis one way or another. At the least, Danzig had be returned and the corridor question settled. If not, Hitler said, there would be war. Soothingly, he added that he was a reasonable man and would be willing to carry out the transfer of the corridor in stages. He then repeated his declaration that there would be war if his demands were not met—and pledged it would be a brutal fight.

Normally, the party leaders would jump up, giving the Hitler salute and even breaking into verses of "Deutschland, Deutschland über Alles." Not this time. The applause was weak and came only when it was obvious the men were expected to respond.

Many of these men were veterans of Nazism, of early ironfisted days. Hitler tried to stir their military ardor, declaring hoarsely he would go to the front lines himself, but their response remained lackluster. The war would be quite difficult, he said, perhaps even hopeless. "As long as I am alive, there will be no talk of capitulation!" he shouted.

Still the reaction was weak.

Hitler kept trying to rouse them. He sought to answer the men's worries, arguing that Italy's refusal to join with them was in Germany's best interest. Yet his audience was passive. Then he took on the most sensitive subject of all, the Communists, whom some of these men had fought in the streets. The party, he said, had misunderstood the pact with the Soviet Union. This, he announced, his voice croaking, was a pact with Satan to drive out the devil. He was not changing the party's anti-Communist policy. Nevertheless, any means at their disposal were justified when dealing with the Russians—even this pact. Again, the applause was tepid.[12]

When he finished, Hitler stood there as the delegates dutifully stretched out their arms to salute him. He walked back down the Long Hall with his entourage, appearing dejected. One of the Reichstag members said later he thought the speech had fallen flat.

Not long after Hitler returned to his apartments in the Old Chancellery, Göring came in saying he had received a call from Dahlerus. The Swede was on his way from London with another message from the British, and they were keeping Henderson in London overnight to await Hitler's reaction to what Dahlerus was bringing. Göring said the Swede would arrive later in the evening. Göring departed promising he would bring Dahlerus's message as soon as the man arrived, and Hitler's hopes rose.[13]

As evening approached, Hitler received a message from Mussolini saying he would keep secret Italy's plan to stay out of the war. "The world will learn instead that Italy has concentrated her forces towards the frontiers of the great democracies," Il Duce had written. He said he had placed on the French border seventeen divisions and twenty-seven Alpine battalions, as well as the border guards. Another two divisions were on their way to Libya. "They will leave the French and British in a state of uncertainty and will confront them with a disposition of forces at least equal to theirs," Mussolini wrote.

At last, Mussolini was coming through with at least something. At the end of his note, Mussolini promised to launch a propaganda campaign depicting Italy and Germany as united, and he was sending workers as Hitler had asked. He concluded by saying, "It is my desire to keep in closest contact with you, Führer, in order to coordinate the action of our two countries and make it conform—in every field." It was a pointed reference to Hitler's secret offer to Britain, a reminder that the two nations were supposed to keep each other informed about everything they did.[14]

When he had delivered the note to Weizsäcker, Attolico had brought another message as well. Mussolini, he had said, was willing, if Hitler agreed, to float a scheme for settling the crisis. Of course, it would hinge on the return of Danzig to Germany. He proposed a conference, such as the one they had held at Munich, where all the involved leaders could discuss the entire Polish question. The ambassador also had suggested that Germany and Poland hold separate talks.[15] That was not what Hitler wanted to hear.

By now, it was midevening, and Hitler went into the chancellery's dining room to hold court over dinner. The room was long, with white walls and, in the center, a round table surrounded by fifteen red armchairs. On one wall hung an immense painting of Aurora, who personified dawn in Greek and Roman mythology, driving through the clouds in her chariot.

As usual, Hitler was dominating the conversation when, shortly after ten o'clock, an urgent message from Weizsäcker interrupted all talk. The French were breaking their agreement and disclosing the gist of Hitler's letter to Daladier. The German embassy had called from Paris to say that Daladier's office had notified it that newsmen had besieged Daladier's office with inquiries after they had seen the German chargé d'affaires visit. Since the diplomat had been delivering Hitler's note, Daladier said he felt obliged to make a short statement, giving reporters the general outline of Hitler's message.

Clearly, the letter would have made for splendid propaganda right before Germany launched its invasion, but Hitler had been cheated of that. He feared that if the Allies and the Poles heard only portions of the letter, he would be made to sound too reasonable. His warning that a horrible war was possible must not go unheard, so he had no alternative but to release the entire letter and to do it immediately, while it had the maximum impact on the media and the public. He told Goebbels to instruct the German press and the government news agency to publicize the letter and ordered that it appear in all German papers the next morning. Since the morning papers were nearing or past their first-edition deadlines, this likely caused disruptions in many newsrooms.[16]

Waiting impatiently to hear from Göring, Hitler returned to his dinner companions. Around midnight, the reichsmarschall walked in, and Hitler went with him into another room.

The British were showing some signs of easing their position, Göring said. Dahlerus had brought word they wanted a settlement and friendship with Germany. With heightened interest, Hitler listened further. The British continued to insist that Hitler open negotiations with Poland. Dahlerus had reported that the British were distrustful of Hitler's promise to respect future borders because of their past experience with Germany—meaning his breach of the Munich Agreement.

Furthermore, Göring said, they would not discuss Germany's lost colonies while the country was on mobilization. But, they had added, once the Germany army stood down, they would be quite willing to open discussions and to do so speedily. On the final point of Hitler's offer to Chamberlain, Dahlerus had reported, the English flatly rejected Hitler's offer of military support, saying that would neither fit into their colonial policy nor serve Britain's interest. Indeed, Hitler obviously had not thought of it, but the English had an empire of subjects and a commonwealth of nations to support them if they needed help. Making the offer had been a mistake, because it was not only useless to the British, but they were able to use it as they sought to undermine Italy's ties with Germany.

There was one other major point they had raised, and it was quite timely, considering the secret protocol Ribbentrop had worked out with Stalin. They insisted, Göring said, that Poland's boundaries be guaranteed by all five of the major European nations—Germany, France, Britain, Italy, and the Soviet Union.

The two men discussed each point as Hitler worked out a reply for Göring to deliver to Dahlerus. Britain's insistence that he negotiate with the Poles was not what Hitler wanted. He sought negotiation with Britain, excluding Poland just as they had excluded Czechoslovakia when they had made that agreement at Munich.

But, Hitler reasoned, perhaps Britain's insistence could be worked to Germany's advantage. If he did agree to sit down with the Poles, it could make him look like he was making a concession, a point he could use as proof that he wanted a peaceful solution to the crisis. The Poles, as he saw it, would never agree to open negotiations with Germany, because Britain's guarantee freed them from any need to negotiate. Nevertheless, Hitler reasoned, if he timed his offer to negotiate so that the Poles would rebuff his overture on the very eve of the invasion, he could claim to Britain and France that the Poles were bringing the war on themselves. And he could put himself in an even more favorable light if he drew up a list of concessions so appealing it would make Germany look as if its demands were quite moderate.

On top of that, if his offer were kept secret until it was too late for the Poles to accept it, he could make them seem even less sympathetic. Perhaps, he thought, this could be the wedge he needed to keep Britain from going to war. So, he said, Göring needed to tell Dahlerus that it was essential that Britain persuade the Poles to begin direct negotiations immediately.

As to the question of Germany's former colonies, Göring should say that Hitler was eager to resolve that question and suspicious of the delay. Hitler requested that he tell Dahlerus he felt Britain was being insincere by delaying those talks. After all, Hitler told Göring, he had brought up the colonial question as simply another issue to explore. He planned to get into any questions about the colonies only after he had resolved the Polish business.

Hitler also instructed Göring to give Dahlerus the impression he was satisfied that Britain really wanted to make a final settlement. He wanted to let them feel that the atmosphere was ripe for negotiations in Berlin and emphasize again the urgency of negotiations with Poland. Then Hitler told Göring to stress once more that he, Hitler, was offering to guarantee the sanctity of the British Empire—a truly ridiculous statement that Hitler still thought would bring support from many Englishmen.

As Göring prepared to leave, Hitler reiterated that Britain needed to understand all this had to be kept secret. He wanted no repeat of what the French had just done.[17]

It now was nearly one thirty in the morning. Once Göring was out the door, Hitler announced he was retiring. The lights in the chancellery went off, and Hitler climbed into bed.[18] The reichsmarschall went to his Berlin mansion and called Dahlerus at his hotel to deliver Hitler's message, setting a positive tone by telling him at the start that the führer was pleased that Britain wanted a peaceful agreement.

11

INTO THE WEE HOURS

GÖRING RAISED DAHLERUS'S EXPECTATIONS WHEN HE REPEATED THE points Hitler had made. If the note Henderson was bringing was like the points Dahlerus had delivered, Göring said, "there is no reason to suppose that we will not be able to reach an agreement."

The Swede said later this was much better than he had hoped, and without delay, he woke George Ogilvie-Forbes, who was in charge of the British embassy in Henderson's absence. No one had told Ogilvie-Forbes of Dahlerus or his mission, and the diplomat was openly skeptical, but that changed when a little over a half hour later, an embassy aide informed Ogilvie-Forbes that they were decoding from London a cable that featured Dahlerus's name. For roughly two hours, Dahlerus sat with Ogilvie-Forbes recounting the response he had received from Göring.

Back at his hotel, Dahlerus took a bath and then headed off again in a government car to give Göring an account of the meeting. He was taken to Göring's private train, parked on a siding north of Berlin. Since they were mobilized, the commands of the armed forces had moved into their wartime headquarters, and this train was his.

Göring greeted Dahlerus in a garish green dressing gown fastened with a jewel buckle. He was quite talkative—too much, in fact. He said that the British embassy staff had been surprised and suspicious when Dahlerus had called them. From that, Dahlerus assumed that the Germans somehow were listening in on the embassy. Göring was violating the first rule of intelligence, which dictates that you not disclose what you know, because your opponent could cut off the flow of information. Most likely, Göring had learned all this from his intercepts of the embassy's telephone. Later, the Swede warned Ogilvie-Forbes that the Germans knew about the staff's comments, but both men thought mistakenly that the information had come from inside the embassy. Ogilvie-Forbes, too, never thought of telephone taps and shrugged off the warning, telling Dahlerus that their technicians had checked the embassy for bugs and the place was clean.[1]

* * *

At last, Hitler had gained enough sleep. The führer arose feeling much more himself, his thoughts clearer, his emotions better held in check. He was feeling more optimistic because he had come up with a new strategy. His hero, Bismarck, had once said that a government had the best chance of winning a war when it convinced its people of the rightness of that war. He would follow that precept.

He began laying out the set of terms to a secretary. First, he would offer to negotiate with the Poles.

When he did, he would repeat the request he had made the previous fall and winter, the one Beck had rejected both times. First, he would ask for the return of Danzig. Next, he would repeat his request for authority to build an autobahn and a railroad across the corridor connecting East Prussia with the rest of Germany. He figured England would be sympathetic to that since the highway and rail line would serve only to reconnect German lands that the Polish Corridor had severed. He reasoned the British would not find the issue of a mere corridor through the Polish Corridor worth fighting for. In addition, the British had seemed friendly to the return of Danzig. Moreover, led by the Nazis, the city-state's voters already had placed Germans in charge of the government there. Not only were these the same basic terms he had offered Beck, but they were requests that, if they went to war, would sound reasonable and right.

He also would propose that they hold plebiscites in the corridor and allow the inhabitants to choose which country they wanted to live in. Surely, Hitler thought, the democratic British with their love of elections and freedom of choice would agree to that point.

Hitler was certain the Poles would never agree to any of this. They already had resisted any negotiations, and to them, it was a matter of national survival that the corridor remain intact and that they have unobstructed access to the Baltic Sea. Moreover, it would be imperative to them that Polish and German minorities who lived along the German border continue under the dominion of Warsaw.

Those points might have appealed to the British, but they would not be well received in Warsaw. Hitler was gambling that Warsaw's reaction would cause the British to lose patience with Poland. Hopefully his offer also would quench the uneasiness of the German public and the Nazi Party leaders who had given his speech such a cool reception.

Hitler set about refining his demands into points, pacing in the apartment's study as he dictated. Finally, he sent his dictation down the street to the foreign ministry.

Soon, Göring called from his train telling Hitler that he had just finished his second session with Dahlerus. Again, he had told the Swede that it was essential for the British to pressure the Poles to come and negotiate. Göring reported he thought he was succeeding in winning Dahlerus's sympathy. That morning, he even had wheeled out his top staff officers to tell the Swede how much they wanted to avoid war.[2]

Hitler gave Göring an outline of the points he was planning to offer and explained his plan to divide the British and the Poles. To make his plan work, he said, he needed one more day, so he was postponing the invasion date—from Thursday until the following day, September 1.[3]

Keitel and Brauchitsch were waiting in the chancellery's conservatory, or sunroom, for Hitler to give them the new date. Hitler already had sent the generals a warning against trying another plot against him, but in case they still harbored such strong misgivings about him, he went out of his way to assure the two that he would keep Britain at peace. He had good reason to be concerned because he had lost face with the army and could not afford another eleventh-hour postponement. Moreover, the invasion had to commence during the first week of September, weeks before the start of Poland's notorious rainy season.

Poland, Hitler said, would reject Germany's offer, and the British would cut off their support. And he showed them a list of the key points he would make to the English. He asked Keitel what he thought. "I find them very moderate," said the general.[4] But as news of his plan reached some of the other officers, their hopes dimmed. "War inevitable unless a miracle happens," Halder noted in his diary.[5]

In the late afternoon, Dietrich gave Hitler his daily press briefing, and one of the items set off alarm bells. There was a press report that the Soviets were withdrawing the troops from the Polish border that they had placed there during the Sudeten crisis. The troops had not been part of Germany's invasion plan—merely a security move by the Russians—but they had put additional pressure on the Poles. To Hitler, the withdrawal could reduce that pressure and possibly mean the Soviets were pulling back from supporting the invasion. Ribbentrop, who had been restored to good graces, came hurrying in, and Hitler sent him off to call the ambassador in Moscow and see whether the Russians were backing away.[6]

Then the führer went off to an early dinner. Henderson was on his way from London, and they would be meeting right in the middle of Hitler's usual dinnertime. Hitler had ordered that the ambassador be received with the full honors accorded a major foreign visitor, and at ten thirty, Henderson's chauffeur drove him into the Court of Honor at the New Reich Chancellery to be greeted by an SS guard of honor and a roll of drums.

Henderson had always worn a red carnation in his buttonhole but several days earlier had gone without one. When a reporter asked him about it, he had said he thought it inappropriate to wear one in a time of such crisis. But tonight he wore a carnation, and as he entered the chancellery, he was greeted by Otto Meissner, the chief of the chancellery, who said he was glad to see that the flower had returned.[7]

Hitler; Ribbentrop, who was relishing his reinstatement, and their interpreter, Schmidt, were standing in Hitler's study when his escort led Henderson in. They sat around the table in front of the hearth, and Henderson handed over Chamberlain's note.

The note avoided any mention of Britain meeting with Germany, thus extinguishing Hitler's hope he could lure the English into mediating the crisis. Instead, Chamberlain described Britain's desire for a lasting friendship and said the British had persuaded the Poles to come and negotiate. The note went on to specify that the negotiations should protect "Poland's essential interests." It did not mention anything about Poland's "rights." It was an interesting choice of words, because what the Poles might view as their "rights" would not necessarily win the support of the British, yet "essential interests" would.

To prevent public opinion from interfering with the talks, Chamberlain urged that news of any mistreatment of minorities be "suppressed," a fire Goebbels had been stoking vigorously. The note concluded by repeating Britain's determination to honor its alliance with the Poles.

The note outlined everything that Dahlerus had reported. Certainly, getting Poland to come and talk was a major step toward what Hitler sought. But Chamberlain did not offer to be the peacemaker as Hitler had wanted.

Henderson reported later to London that Hitler was calmer than usual and seemed more receptive to what Chamberlain had said. At one point, as if reading Hitler's mind, the ambassador hinted at what London would support by reminding Hitler of his request months earlier for the auto and rail corridor to East Prussia and saying the English would never agree to eliminating the Polish Corridor itself.

Having drunk a half bottle of champagne while waiting for the letter to be translated into German, Henderson was quite voluble. In fact, he took over most of the conversation. When Hitler asked whether Britain would agree to an alliance with Germany, Henderson said that he, personally, did not think it impossible. That statement reportedly breached his instructions, upsetting senior officials in London's foreign office.

Toward the end of the meeting, Hitler told Henderson that he could not give him an answer until he had studied the note thoroughly. Turning to Ribbentrop, he added, "We must summon Reichsmarschall Göring to discuss it with him"—words that must have rankled the foreign minister.

Chamberlain's note stirred optimism in a number of quarters. When Dahlerus visited the British embassy that afternoon, he had found Ogilvie-Forbes, who was decoding some of the cables from London, to be in high spirits. After Henderson's meeting with Hitler, Göring sent word to Dahlerus that the prospects of peace were at their best, and the mood was similar among the senior staff at the German foreign ministry.[8]

On Henderson's departure, Göring did join them, and he found Hitler quiet. To Ribbentrop, he seemed pensive. Apparently, Hitler felt that by avoiding an offer to intervene, Chamberlain had put him in a corner. Nevertheless, as Hitler continued to think over Chamberlain's message, he seemed to grow more optimistic. Chamberlain had promised that a Polish emissary would come. Even though it would have been better to have the British serve as arbitrators and lose patience with the Poles, Hitler decided talks between the Germans and the Poles might achieve the same thing. The Poles would not agree to Germany's demands just as they would have balked if Britain had been mediating. Moreover, Henderson had mentioned Hitler's request for a corridor across the corridor, a definite indication Britain would buy that proposal even if the Poles rejected it.

That gave Hitler hope. Perhaps they could get from the British what they wanted after all. The messages Dahlerus had taken to London seemed to have borne fruit. "So you still believe that Dahlerus is a British agent?" Hitler asked mockingly of Ribbentrop. The foreign minister was not amused.[9]

But that did not keep Ribbentrop from pushing his stand-tough strategy. It seemed to him the British note could persuade the Poles to negotiate. If that should happen, he argued, the Germans should make demands so outrageous the Poles would reject them. Henderson had warned against such an attempt, but Ribbentrop was insistent regardless.

Into the wee hours, Hitler was pulled back and forth by Ribbentrop and Göring, who urged Hitler to go back to the moderate offer he had embraced only hours before. "Let's drop the all-or-nothing game," the reichsmarschall said. But Hitler replied, "All my life I have played for all or nothing."[10]

Ribbentrop and Göring kept pulling at him, swinging Hitler back and forth between friendship with Britain and the risk of a world war.

* * *

In Warsaw, the government grew more nervous. Nazi mobs were attacking Poles on the streets of Danzig, and the victims were being arrested and jailed for creating a public disturbance. German railway workers were staying home from work, and Polish warehouses were blocked from shipping exports. More ominous, the German battleship *Schleswig Holstein*, which was making a courtesy call to Danzig, had overstayed its scheduled departure. Moreover, the ship had moved down the harbor and was sitting off the Westerplatte, where the Poles had a military depot.[11]

12

A SHOUTING MATCH

GÖRING WENT HOME BELIEVING HE HAD PREVAILED. BETWEEN his efforts with Hitler and Dahlerus's talks in London, he was certain there would be no war. At about eleven o'clock Tuesday morning, Dahlerus went to see Göring at his Leipziger Platz town house. The reichsmarschall went out to see him, rushed across the room, and grabbed the Swede by the hand, saying excitedly, "We'll have peace. Peace has been assured."[1]

As soon as they finished their meeting, Dahlerus went straight to the British embassy, now convinced more than ever that Hitler would avoid war. He told Henderson that he had come from seeing Göring and that Hitler now realized Britain was not bluffing.[2]

* * *

But Göring's optimism was on shaky ground. Ribbentrop was revising the draft of the note to Chamberlain that Hitler had sent to the foreign ministry staff. The moderate offers Hitler had shown to Keitel were no more. Ribbentrop had remade them into a set of tougher demands on Poland. As Weizsäcker had noted in his diary, Ribbentrop was killing any chance of a workable solution.

The revised demands included the return of Danzig, to which Britain was sympathetic. But there were other points that the British would be most unlikely to support. Instead of asking for a rail and highway corridor across the Polish Corridor or a plebiscite to determine its ownership, the revised list demanded return of the corridor itself and the exchange of Germans living in Poland for Poles living in the corridor. Ribbentrop had persuaded Hitler that he would never regain the corridor through a vote of the inhabitants because so many Germans had moved away. The corridor now was populated largely by Poles.

Hitler's scheme was quite simple. If the Poles were to fulfill their promise to negotiate, they would need to send their emissary the next day, August 30. Since the Poles would never agree to Hitler's terms, the emissary would turn down the Germans' offer on August 31. Hitler would then tell Britain the Poles were unwilling to compromise, and his army would march into Poland the following day, September 1.

The British had insisted they stand behind their pledge to Poland, but Ribbentrop was good at persuading his führer that it was only talk. Once again, he told Hitler that the English were soft and would never back up their promise. He insisted that Germany could drive such a wedge between the Poles and the English that Britain would desert Poland.[3] Hitler listened, ignoring Göring's warnings and turning more and more to the idea of risking war.

Meanwhile, the führer received disturbing news from Otto Dietrich. The London papers were reporting that Italy might remain neutral if Germany went to war against Poland. The Germans were convinced the Italians had leaked the story, but it apparently came from the British government itself. Unbeknownst to the Germans, Ciano complained of the stories to the British ambassador, saying they made Italy look like it was deserting Hitler and that the stories could anger Mussolini so much he might join the Germans after all.[4]

Early in the afternoon, Ribbentrop came in to say that Attolico had just visited him. The ambassador had said that Mussolini was considering a proposal to bring Germany and Poland together. He was not proposing an international conference such as the session they had held in Munich. Instead, he himself would sit down with the Poles and the Germans and try to mediate a solution.

Hitler wanted none of this. It would delay the invasion again, leaving too little time for them to conquer the country before the rainy season. Ribbentrop said he had told Attolico that matters had gone too far for such a meeting. Hitler, he had said, was determined to settle the crisis himself, one way or another. The Wehrmacht already was on the march.[5]

In late afternoon, Dietrich informed Hitler that Chamberlain had addressed Parliament and his words had echoed the agreeable tone of his note. That seemed a favorable omen, but Hitler's mind was set. The führer had been truthful when he had told Göring that he had always sought all or nothing, and this evening, he planned to do precisely that. Ribbentrop had taken over drafting the note to Chamberlain, and since Hitler liked playing

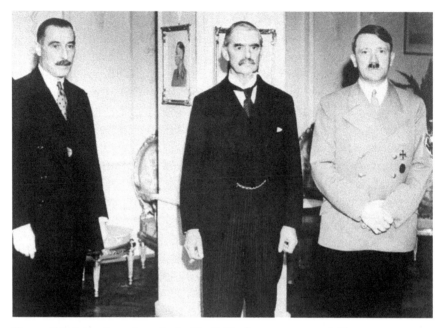

Fig. 12.1. Britain's ambassador to Berlin, Nevile Henderson, accompanied his prime minister, Neville Chamberlain (*center*), to the ill-fated meeting with Hitler in Godesburg that led to the Munich conference.

the tough guy, he was ignoring Göring's warnings and would go along gladly with Ribbentrop's prose.

Henderson came in wearing another carnation, and they all sat by the fireplace in the circle around the coffee table. Schmidt was there as well, although he had little to do because Henderson insisted on speaking in German. The note they handed Henderson did not contain any of the offers Hitler had shown Keitel. Those offers would have opened the door for an agreement. Henderson had come hoping for an accord and believing there was a faint hope they could achieve one. Indeed, the first three paragraphs fueled that hope further, but as Henderson read on, his hopes began to fade.

Trying to drive in the wedge between Britain and Poland, Ribbentrop had inserted the usual litany of accusations and complaints against Poland. Germans were being mistreated, Henderson read. Danzig's borders had been closed, it charged and complained of "barbaric actions of maltreatment."

Then the note grew darker. Germany, it said, no longer agreed that negotiations could end the crisis. When Germany had tried to negotiate, the Poles had rebuffed the country, Ribbentrop had written.

Germany, the note continued, would negotiate as the British wanted, giving Henderson's spirits cause to edge up. It went on to say Germany would agree to receive a Polish emissary who was empowered to negotiate. That sounded good. But then Henderson read more of Ribbentrop's material: "They count on the arrival of this emissary on Wednesday, the 30th of August, 1939."

They were giving the Poles only twenty-four hours to negotiate!

Until then, Henderson had read in silence, and Hitler, Ribbentrop, and Schmidt had sat watching him. But reading those words outraged him, and he looked up at Hitler.

"This sounds like an ultimatum," he said. "The Poles are given barely twenty-four hours to make their plans."

Not true, Hitler said heatedly. Hitler and Ribbentrop explained that the armies were already facing each other. The Poles had mobilized, and they had killed Germans, the two claimed.

"The time is short," Hitler said, "because there is the danger that fresh provocation may result in the outbreak of fighting."

Henderson said that the British might not be able to get a Polish negotiator to Berlin that quickly.

Hitler replied that it took only an hour and a half to fly from Warsaw to Berlin.

Then, with both his voice and temper rising, Hitler went on. This was no ultimatum, he said. He had set the deadline to emphasize the urgency of the moment. The Poles had mobilized, he repeated, adding, "My soldiers are asking me yes or no." He maintained the Poles were massacring Germans, and his voice rose higher: "You do not care how many Germans are being slaughtered in Poland!"

Hitler had done it. To Henderson, he and his fellow Englishmen respected the lives of others. That was why they were trying to avoid a war. To him, Hitler's accusation was a blatant insult. It was not only an aspersion on the British people but an affront to him personally. More important, it gave the ambassador the opportunity to treat Hitler with the same tough talk that he used on Henderson and others he tried to bully.

"I will not listen to such language from you or anybody," Henderson roared, surprising both Hitler and Ribbentrop. Henderson shouted that the accusation was typical of Hitler's exaggerations. Raising his voice yet higher, the usually mild-mannered ambassador continued to shout Germany's führer into silence.

Ribbentrop and Schmidt sat stunned. Since becoming ambassador, Henderson said, he had done all he could to avoid war. Now it was Hitler's choice—and he punctuated his statement by banging his fist on the coffee table's glass top.

Hitler's face turned red, and suddenly, they were in a shouting match.

Their shouts grew louder. Henderson told Hitler that if he wanted war, he would have it, and if so, Britain would outlast Germany.

The Poles had mobilized and were killing more Germans, Hitler said once more. Any talks with Poland could never succeed, he maintained.

It was his choice. Whether they succeeded or failed would depend on Hitler's own good will, Henderson thundered, glaring at him.

Henderson stood to walk out, and Hitler, realizing he was losing his chance to charm the British, would not rise and give him leave. Henderson, who did not want to create an incident, sat back down, and in a normal voice, Hitler tried to calm the situation by saying again that the deadline was not an ultimatum. He began to talk about Germany's desire for friendship. He had had many English friends, he said, and wanted only peace with Britain.

Henderson finally told him he would transmit the note immediately and asked whether the Polish emissary would be treated as an equal.

"Certainly," Hitler replied.[6]

Henderson left dejected. He had hoped his shouts would pressure the führer to stop his blustering and be more reasonable. But his tactic had backfired. It had made Hitler angrier.

As he was being escorted to his car, he told Meissner that he might never wear his carnation again in Germany.[7] His despondence had been made all the worse when he had found a group of officers, all in uniform and led by Keitel and Brauchitsch, standing outside Hitler's door.[8] Hitler might have ordered them to wait there in hopes of giving the ambassador the impression the army was ready to march.

Back at the embassy, Henderson cabled his boss, Lord Halifax, in London that he had shouted at Hitler deliberately. "I thought for once Hitler must be given a dose of his own medicine," he wrote. He had considered the idea earlier and decided it "might do some good."[9]

* * *

In Rome, Mussolini had been fretting, wanting to do something. As Ciano had feared, the reports in the British press that Italy might remain neutral had fired him up. He was even talking of military moves. That deepened Ciano's concern, and he had persuaded Mussolini to send a message to Hitler urging him to negotiate with the Poles.[10]

Not long after Henderson's departure, Attolico appeared, bearing Mussolini's note. Attolico also delivered an oral message from Mussolini saying he had good relations with the British and would be happy to help Hitler either politically or through diplomacy.

His anger already fired up by the stormy session with Henderson and what he considered Italy's duplicity four days earlier, Hitler was notably inhospitable to the ambassador, telling him he already was about to negotiate with a Polish representative and needed no help. And with that, he dismissed Attolico frostily.[11]

After everyone had left, Hitler was sitting in his study brooding over Henderson's performance when his photographer friend Heinrich Hoffmann dropped in. Hoffmann, who rarely expressed his opinion on government policy, broke his rule and told Hitler he was concerned they would have war with Britain.

"Don't you believe it!" Hitler said. "England is bluffing!" Then he grinned impishly, which he rarely did. "And so am I!"[12]

He was misleading Hoffmann. He was not bluffing, and he was wrong about the British as well. Unfortunately, despite Göring's optimism, Hitler still did not comprehend that the British were far from bluffing. In fact, they were losing any hopes they might have had about Hitler. The next morning, Henderson telegraphed London that if Hitler could not get what he wanted by peaceful means, he would try to take it by force. This was a new view for Henderson. If they allowed Hitler to have his way, he said, it would only mean another victory such as the one he had won at Munich and another showdown in a year or two. Obviously, the ambassador, who had always been conciliatory toward the Germans, had lost all patience.[13]

Hoffmann went off with Hitler to the Old Chancellery, where some of the führer's old friends, all early Nazi followers, were assembling for an evening of talk and dinner. Besides Hoffmann, the group included Ribbentrop; Göring; and Hitler's deputy, Rudolf Hess, a strange, mystical man whose appearance was quite rare at chancellery gatherings. Hitler told Hess of his confrontation with Henderson and described in detail how the ambassador had banged his fist on the table. He had almost thrown the man out, Hitler told Hess. Already incensed, Hitler grew increasingly belligerent as he recounted the meeting. Now he wanted to invade. As the evening wore on, Hitler's anger continued to rise. Finally, he declared, "In two months, Poland will be finished, and then we shall have a great peace conference with the western powers."[14]

* * *

Göring was outraged. To him, Ribbentrop was undermining all his work. Moreover, the British ambassador has caused the führer to be more resolute. Hitler seemed to have forgotten Göring's entreaties for an agreement with Britain. The reichsmarschall was able to get the führer aside long enough to ask him to allow Göring to make one more attempt with Dahlerus. Hitler agreed, telling Göring to have Dahlerus persuade the British that the tension between the two countries was so intense it was imperative that a Polish envoy appear in Berlin the next day. He suggested they dangle the prospect of a plebiscite in front of them because telephone intercepts had revealed that the foreign ministry in Warsaw had told Lipski, the Polish ambassador, to be receptive to such an idea. That, Hitler thought, might help the British lure the Poles to the bargaining table.[15]

Göring went off to his town house on the Leipziger Platz and called Dahlerus. The Swede was at the Esplanade Hotel with the British embassy counsel, Ogilvie-Forbes, discussing the confrontation between Henderson and Hitler. Forbes was telling the Swede that the situation seemed so grave it looked almost hopeless. He declared that there was little point in negotiating further with the Germans. As soon as the call came, Dahlerus left Ogilvie-Forbes and went off to see Göring.

He found the reichsmarschall angry. Like Henderson, Göring had lost patience with the other side. The meeting had upset him as it had Ogilvie-Forbes. To him, Henderson's loss of temper had threatened to destroy all his efforts at keeping peace. Göring declared that Henderson's shouting and table thumping proved that the British really did not want to come to any agreement. He took a copy of the note and underlined key passages in red pencil, including the requirement that the Polish representative come the next day. They had not issued an ultimatum, the reichsmarschall said, insisting that the note to Chamberlain had been friendly. Then he began rehashing all Germany's grievances against the British. To Dahlerus, he had totally reversed the view of England he had held in their recent meetings.

Dahlerus said later that they had never discussed the Poles before, only the corridor and Danzig, but now Göring did. The deadline in the note, Göring said, reflected Germany's doubt of Poland's true intentions. "We know the Poles," he suddenly said, launching into a tirade against them, their policies, and their treatment of the Germans who lived there. Germany no longer could put up with it, he said, claiming that Germany's armed forces were mobilized as a precaution against the Poles. "Sixty German divisions are there waiting," he said. "We all hope that nothing will happen, that military action between Poland and Germany will not become necessary." But given how tense the situation was, he added, "We are compelled to insist that a settlement be reached without delay."

Göring started in on the Poles again. "The Poles are mad. Their treatment of their German minority is inexplicable and inhuman."[16] Germany, he said, would have declared war on Poland if it had not wanted to forge an agreement with Britain. Meanwhile, the Poles were encouraged to provoke the Germans because they were backed by their mutual assistance pact with Britain.

Dahlerus began to think his cause was gone. If Hitler, he thought, was in the same frame of mind, all was lost. But soon, the reichsmarschall began to soften. He had something to tell Dahlerus, but in utmost confidence. Hitler was putting together for Poland what Göring termed "a generous offer." That, he argued, made the confrontation with Henderson all the more regrettable. Then he dropped Hitler's plebiscite bait. And he repeated the claim for a railroad and highway corridor through the corridor, saying if the plebiscite resulted in Germany getting the Polish Corridor, Poland would have a similar roadway and rail line through it to the port of Danzig.

It was roughly two in the morning. Their meeting had been going on for nearly three hours when Göring urged Dahlerus to fly to London and stress again Germany's desire for an agreement with Britain. He asked that Dahlerus tell them in confidence that the next day, Hitler planned to present Poland with a note containing conditions so favorable both Poland and England should agree to them.

As Dahlerus prepared to depart, the reichsmarschall thanked him for what he had been doing. It was out of character, and surprised, Dahlerus said they doubtless would be meeting again soon. But Göring grew serious and said, "Perhaps, but certain people are doing what they can to prevent you from getting out of this alive." With that, he bade Dahlerus farewell.[17]

13

"WHERE IS THE POLE?"

D AHLERUS'S MEETINGS BACK AND FORTH HAD BEEN CLOAKED in secrecy, but somehow rumors had sprung up. He flew out of Berlin at five o'clock the next morning, and a few hours later, he landed at a little-used airfield outside London. As he was driven through Hyde Park on his way to a discreet side entrance of the British foreign office, Dahlerus was astounded to see newspaper signboards announcing that a "mysterious airplane" had taken off from Berlin at five o'clock.

Soon after Dahlerus's arrival, Alexander Cadogan, the foreign office's undersecretary, escorted him out the back way and across to 10 Downing Street, where Neville Chamberlain and Cadogan's superior, Lord Halifax, were waiting. It was ten thirty London time Wednesday morning, August 30. Göring's fears were confirmed. The mood there and back across the street at the foreign office made it plain to Dahlerus that everyone had lost patience with Hitler. In fact, Chamberlain questioned the use of any further negotiation.

Dahlerus suggested they urge the Polish government to refrain from any action that might inflame the crisis, handing Chamberlain a list of four points that he recommended the Poles follow. He also asked Chamberlain to convey the four points to the Polish government, which Halifax did later that day.

Dahlerus went on to relay Göring's message that Hitler was preparing a proposal for Poland. Chamberlain and Halifax were wary, saying it was a ploy to delay things, or Hitler had misled Göring, or the reichsmarschall had lied. But Dahlerus insisted Göring had said it was to be ready that day, suggesting that he let the reichsmarschall himself prove it.

With that, Cadogan took Dahlerus back to his office, where the Swede phoned Göring. Eager to hear whether Dahlerus had undone the damage

Hitler and Ribbentrop had created, the reichsmarschall came to the phone immediately. Hitler was drafting his note, he assured them, and the terms would be more generous to Poland than he had said they would be. In fact, he added, he was nearly certain Hitler would suggest a plebiscite in the corridor. Hitler planned to say that after the plebiscite decided which country owned which pieces of land, the minorities who would be left there could move. Any Poles left in lands Germany would occupy would be released from any military obligations.

Dahlerus then suggested sending the note to Warsaw through Lipski, and Göring sounded as if that would be all right.

Dahlerus told the reichsmarschall that he assumed Hitler would have the terms ready by evening.

"The führer is on it," Göring replied, adding that they all needed to move quickly. It was now approaching two in the afternoon in Berlin, and there was no sign from Warsaw that an emissary was on his way.

Back the two went to 10 Downing, where everyone gathered in the Cabinet Room and Cadogan confirmed what the reichsmarschall had said. Dahlerus went on to describe in detail the terms that Göring had laid out the night before and repeated what Göring had told him on the phone.

It turned out that the British leaders were especially skeptical since Hitler was demanding that the Poles come to Berlin. Hácha had done that the previous spring only to surrender Czechoslovakia. After some discussion, Chamberlain told Dahlerus to return to Berlin while the cabinet met to consider its response to Hitler's note. He instructed him to assure the Germans that the British wanted to help end the crisis but that they would not encourage the Poles to negotiate in Berlin.

Finally, Chamberlain dismissed Dahlerus, saying the cabinet was to decide on the matter and Dahlerus should get back to Berlin. He added that when he arrived, Dahlerus should check in with the British embassy for news of the decision.

With that, Cadogan took Dahlerus back to his office, where the state secretary, still concerned about the way Hitler had dictated his demands to Hácha, asked the Swede to call Göring again and make certain Hitler was not laying out his terms in the form of a demand. The reichsmarschall assured him there were no demands. It all was being worded as a "basis for discussion." But, Göring added, it was essential that someone come from Warsaw to receive the proposals.

Dahlerus and Cadogan talked some more. Soon, it was approaching four in the afternoon in Berlin and Warsaw and still no sign the Poles were preparing to send an emissary.

Grasping again at the hope they could avoid a repeat of Hácha's surrender and simultaneously lure the Poles to the conference table, Cadogan told Dahlerus that the British were not about to suggest that the Poles meet in Berlin. Perhaps, he suggested, the meeting could be held at some neutral site. Once again, Dahlerus telephoned the reichsmarschall.

Through the day, Hitler's desire for war grew. He already had told the Wehrmacht to prepare for an invasion in two days' time, on Friday, September 1, and if they had to delay, it would be for only one day.[1] Furthermore, he was more insistent that the Poles come to Berlin. Cadogan's suggestion that they meet on neutral ground would have angered Hitler, so when Dahlerus forwarded Cadogan's suggestion, Göring grew irritated. "Nonsense!" he exclaimed in his shrill voice. "The negotiations must take place in Berlin, where Hitler has his headquarters." He added with a tone of finality, "I can see no reason why the Poles should find it difficult to send emissaries to Berlin."[2]

The sun now was beginning to edge down in the western sky and still no word of the Polish emissaries. On that somber note, Dahlerus prepared to fly back to Berlin. To keep his trip secret, Kingsley Wood, Britain's air minister, had arranged to have the plane moved from the insignificant airfield where he had landed to an even less noticeable installation used for testing new aircraft.[3]

In Berlin, Hitler was dictating the sixteen-point list of concessions and demands the Germans would present to the Polish emissary. As accommodating as they might seem, Chamberlain was right to be skeptical. Hitler was not as serious as the concessions sounded. Despite the offer, he planned to sabotage the talks when the Poles sent their negotiator. He confided afterward, "I needed an alibi, especially with the German people, to show them that I had done everything to maintain peace. That explains my generous offer about the settlement of the Danzig and Corridor questions."[4]

Meanwhile, Henderson had delivered a preliminary response from London to the German foreign ministry. It said they were considering Hitler's message but offered little hope they could persuade the Poles to send an envoy on such short notice. "The German government," the message read, "must not expect otherwise."[5]

Moreover, while German intercepts disclosed that Henderson had urged Lipski to have negotiators travel to Berlin that day, they also showed that Lipski was cool to the idea. Warsaw was reluctant to meet Hitler's deadline, the transmissions revealed, because it would make the Poles look as if they were caving in to German demands.[6]

None of that dimmed Göring's hopes for a meeting, but Hitler's deadline for the invasion was drawing closer.

Meanwhile, Hitler had laid out the sixteen-point offer, and the foreign ministry was polishing the draft. Its terms gave new hope to such moderates in the ministry as Schmidt and Weizsäcker. "When I saw the proposals I could scarcely believe my eyes," Schmidt wrote later. "We work out a reasonable compromise plan, the first constructive idea in months," Weizsäcker recorded in his diary. "But is it only 'for show'?"[7]

Listed was the idea of a plebiscite that Göring had mentioned to Dahlerus. The first point was a demand that Danzig be returned, but the second point suggested that the occupants of the corridor itself vote on which country they wanted to be part of. If Poland won the plebiscite in the corridor, Germany would receive a corridor of its own with an autobahn and a railroad that linked Germany with East Prussia and Danzig. If the Germans were to win the vote, Poland would have a similar corridor to the sea at Gdynia, which would remain Polish.[8] It all seemed most reasonable, and if Hitler had been serious in his offer and given the Poles and the British time to study it, he probably could have split the British from their support if the Poles had gone on refusing to talk.

At four thirty Berlin time, Goebbels's press office announced that a meeting of the cabinet was convening at the chancellery. The Associated Press relayed the announcement to much of the world.[9] But what the world did not know was that Hitler had no cabinet. It was a move to make Hitler more determined, and the announcement had its intended impact and raised the level of tension.

At five thirty, the tension worsened when the embassy in Warsaw phoned the foreign ministry in Berlin reporting that notices had been posted in Poland ordering general mobilization. It would be effective the next day.[10] Not good news for Göring.

Ribbentrop was happy, and it gave him all the more leverage to egg Hitler on. In fact, Ribbentrop said later that this excited Hitler, and he began to listen avidly to news reports of incidents between Poles and Germans in Poland that the German propaganda machine was claiming.[11]

On his side, following up on the suggestion Dahlerus had made in his second call, Göring pressed Hitler to forget the idea of giving his proposal to emissaries from Warsaw and instead allow the Polish ambassador to receive it. So far, Göring was getting nowhere.

At his afternoon briefing, Hitler received more news that would increase the pressure on the Poles. TASS, the Soviet news agency, reported that Russia was placing more troops on the Polish border.[12] That further encouraged Ribbentrop, who continued to assure the führer that the British would never go to war.

Hitler instructed Göring to prepare a decree creating a war cabinet. It would be called the Ministerial Council for Reich Defense, and Göring would head it. Members would include Rudolf Hess and Keitel.[13] Hitler told Goebbels he was to announce the decree at midnight, after the Poles had missed their deadline. Hopefully that would convince Britain all the more that Hitler was serious.

Meanwhile, Hitler ordered the high command to continue its invasion preparations for Friday, September 1. Apparently thinking he could still use diplomacy to hold back the English, Hitler added that they would postpone the operation until Saturday in the event they requested to extend negotiations.[14]

In the British view, the chance of bringing Hitler together with Polish representatives was slimmer than ever. That morning, Howard Kennard, Britain's ambassador in Warsaw, had cabled the foreign office and said he saw no way to persuade the Polish leaders to send a representative to Berlin by Hitler's deadline. Kennard and the Poles had no idea what the sixteen-point proposal contained, but, the ambassador said, knowing they had turned down the idea of a corridor across the corridor the preceding spring, there was no chance they would agree to whatever the Germans were now proposing. Rather than be treated like Lithuania when Hitler seized Memel or Hácha and Austria's Kurt Schuschnigg, "They would certainly sooner fight and perish rather than submit to such humiliation," he declared.[15]

Without question, Hitler's policy of browbeating countries into submission had backfired. No one trusted him. The British had lost patience with him, suspecting that whatever he did would be a repeat of what he had done to those nations.

Yet even at the last minute, Hitler was still gambling, thinking he somehow could lure the English into putting pressure on the Poles or at the least refusing to back them on the battlefield. Perhaps, he thought, Chamberlain would turn cool to the Poles if he saw the sixteen-point proposal. So he ordered that a copy, classified Secret for the moment, be transmitted to the German embassy in London. It was to be held until Hitler decided whether he wanted it presented.[16]

That evening, with no Polish emissary yet in sight, Ribbentrop received notice from Henderson that he had two messages to deliver to the führer. Henderson had been scheduled to call at eleven thirty that evening, but at the last moment, the embassy received a further message, Britain's response to the note Hitler had given Henderson the previous day. Since it had to be deciphered, Henderson asked for more time, and the meeting was delayed until midnight, the deadline by which the Polish representative was to have arrived.[17] Henderson was told to deliver it to the foreign office rather than go to the Reich Chancellery. Hitler would not see him.

The Poles were missing the deadline. Hitler and Ribbentrop were together in the chancellery exulting. They were fired up. And they were encouraging each other. They now could claim that Poland did not want to negotiate. Ribbentrop had convinced his führer that there would be no war, only a victorious invasion. The British would back off, he said. Holding back for the moment on his idea of presenting Chamberlain with the proposal, Hitler told Ribbentrop he could tell Henderson only what the proposals contained. He had drawn it up only for discussions with the Poles, who had not appeared. He ordered Ribbentrop not to give him the document.[18]

Ribbentrop returned next door to the foreign ministry visibly excited, his face pale, eyes shining, and lips set. He greeted Henderson with marked coldness, without the usual diplomat's cordiality.[19] He maintained an icy look on his face and a distant formality in his words. Sitting between them was Paul Schmidt, the interpreter. Apparently trying to be friendly, Henderson spoke some in German, but that did not break the ice.[20]

Henderson began by saying his country could probably persuade the Poles to avoid any "acts of provocation" but that the Germans must show the same restraint. That set Ribbentrop off. "The Poles are the aggressors, not we!" he said. "You have come to the wrong address."

Henderson told Ribbentrop Britain could not advise Poland to come to Berlin in one day. It was "unreasonable" for the Germans to expect a Polish representative to come so soon and without having some idea what the Germans were proposing to discuss.

"The time is up," Ribbentrop said. "Where is the Pole your government was to provide?"

Henderson recommended he share the proposals with the British government, and if they found Hitler's offering reasonable, Britain would push the Poles to negotiate.

The session was growing stormier by the minute. When Henderson suggested he and Hitler follow normal diplomatic protocol and deliver the proposal to the Polish ambassador, Ribbentrop exploded. "That is out of the question after what has happened!" he shouted. "We demand that a negotiator empowered by his government with full authority should come here to Berlin." All the British had achieved trying to mediate the crisis was Poland's mobilization, Ribbentrop said, his voice full of disdain.

Almost every time Henderson said anything, Ribbentrop would jump up, fold his arms across his chest, and ask flatly whether the ambassador had anything more to say. Indeed he did, Henderson would reply.

While Ribbentrop was savoring his perceived triumph over the Poles, Henderson was tense as he tried as best he could to avoid war, and his temper began to show. The ambassador's face turned red, and his hands trembled as he read Ribbentrop the latest message from London.[21] It said little new, summing up the status of their negotiations and concluding by urging the Germans to promise not to take any military action. If they did, Britain would persuade the Poles to do likewise. That set Ribbentrop off once more. He interrupted Henderson, declaring, "That's an unheard-of suggestion." Crossing his arms, he glared defiantly at the ambassador and shouted "Have you anymore to say!"

Henderson said yes. The British government had obtained information that the Germans were engaging in sabotage in Poland.

Ribbentrop was enraged. "That's a damned lie of the Polish government!"

That fired up Henderson, who shook his finger at Ribbentrop, saying, "You have just said 'damned.' That's no word for a statesman to use in a grave situation."

Outraged that he was being lectured by this Englishman, Ribbentrop jumped up again. "What did you say?"

Henderson jumped up too, and the two stood like fighters glaring at each other.

Normally, when both stood, protocol required that Schmidt, who was of lesser rank, get up as well, but he was so fearful the two would come to blows he remained seated and pretended to go on taking notes. Both men stood there breathing heavily while Schmidt sat between them fearing one would hit the other. At last, Ribbentrop sat, and Henderson slowly followed.

Their tempers better under control, they continued talking until Ribbentrop finally read Henderson the sixteen-point proposal. When he finished and Henderson asked for a copy, Ribbentrop stuck to Hitler's orders and put it in his pocket, refusing to give it to him.[22]

The ambassador left dejected. Any negotiations seemed impossible.[23] Later, he cabled Lord Halifax that Ribbentrop had been "aping Herr Hitler at his worst." As Henderson saw it, any hope for peace had pretty well vanished. His despair deepened when he discovered that while he and Ribbentrop had been meeting, the Germans had announced the creation of the defense council.[24]

But before reporting to London, Henderson had called Lipski, who had come immediately to the embassy. It now was two in the morning. Leaving out the more acrimonious details of his meeting, Henderson reported that the Germans had drawn up their proposals, including the return of Danzig to Germany and a plebiscite in the corridor. It seemed fairly reasonable, he said, urging Lipski to press his bosses in Warsaw to send a negotiator. Henderson recommended he have the negotiator meet with Göring, as dealing with Ribbentrop would be impossible.[25]

For his part, Göring was still trying to woo the British through Dahlerus. When the Swede had arrived back in Berlin that evening, he had been driven out to the reichsmarschall's private railway car, where Göring was waiting in the drawing room. When he had left Göring the night before, the reichsmarschall had been on edge, but this evening, Dahlerus found him calm and composed. In fact, Göring, who knew only that Ribbentrop and Henderson were supposed to meet, was unaware of their confrontation. After Dahlerus briefed Göring on his sessions in London, the reichsmarschall said he had an important piece of information for him, explaining that Ribbentrop was supposed to have given Henderson the proposal. With that, Göring read out the sixteen points. That heartened Dahlerus as it had Göring. Dahlerus then telephoned Ogilvie-Forbes at the British embassy for news on the meeting, but to his surprise, Ogilvie-Forbes told him of Henderson's disastrous collision with Ribbentrop. More talk with the Germans was useless, Ogilvie-Forbes said.

Dahlerus repeated the news to Göring. "If Ribbentrop is going to take every chance of sabotaging attempts to reach an agreement, nothing that you or I can do is going to help," he said. If Göring wanted to bring the British to an agreement, he needed to undo Ribbentrop's damage. He had to pass on to the British the sixteen points. "You yourself have stressed the fairness of the note," he added. "It is only right that the British government be allowed to see it."

Dahlerus urged Göring to let him phone the points to Ogilvie-Forbes. His hands clasped behind him, Göring paced back and forth. The news took him by surprise. He seemed to be pondering whether he should violate Hitler's order to Ribbentrop. Then he came to a quick halt and looked at Dahlerus. "I'll do it. I'll take the responsibility. You can telephone him."

When Dahlerus reached Ogilvie-Forbes, he began reading out the points slowly, but Göring grew nervous and urged him to hurry. He wanted the phone call to be as brief as possible. Göring appeared concerned that Ribbentrop might get word of the call and cause trouble. The call over, Göring provided Dahlerus with a sleeping compartment, insisting he stay there since he had had little sleep the past two days. In the morning, he had the Swede write out the sixteen points and take the list to Henderson so there would be no question whether the ambassador had a correct copy.[26]

Henderson immediately sent a copy to Lipski, who spent the morning talking on the phone to Warsaw. Finally, Henderson sent a message to the German foreign ministry saying London asked that Ribbentrop receive Lipski.[27]

14

THE INTERCEPTED TELEGRAM

O N THE MORNING OF AUGUST 31, ARMY TRUCKS, motorcycles, and even artillery moved about the streets of Berlin. On the roofs, soldiers manned their antiaircraft guns. Somewhere an air-raid siren wailed.[1] Hitler was giving the diplomats a dramatic and foreboding show.

Weizsäcker grew frantic as his outlook for peace turned bleaker. Early that morning, he met with Ulrich von Hassell, and the two diplomats shared their concerns. "We are under no obligation to plunge into the abyss on account of two madmen," Weizsäcker said.[2] He told Hassell that the two men most able to prevent war were Göring and Henderson, and he urged that his friend talk with both. He added that Hassell should point out to Göring that when war came, his beloved estate, Carinhall, would "go up in flames."[3]

At one time, Henderson and Hassell had both been posted in Belgrade and were friends. Hassell went to the embassy, where he found Henderson eating a late breakfast. He told Hassell he had been up much of the night. Hassell urged him to keep pressing Lipski, and Henderson told him he had talked with the ambassador during the night and would keep on working on him. But, he added, the Germans could not keep on treating the Poles like stupid schoolboys whom they could order around. Britain and Germany could reach an agreement, he added, but never if Ribbentrop were involved.

Then Hassell called on Göring's sister, Olga Riegele, telling her how dire the crisis had become and asking her to arrange a meeting with the reichsmarschall. Hearing how serious matters were, she broke into tears and told Hassell how Göring had put his arm around her, saying, "Now you see? Everybody is for war, only I, the soldier and field marshal, am not."[4]

Still in tears, she called her brother at his railway car and put Hassell on the phone. When Hassell said he believed Henderson was doing all he could to keep the peace, Göring was skeptical, complaining he had been "snooty" in his meeting with Ribbentrop, which likely was the version of the confrontation Ribbentrop had given Hitler. That probably was not intended, Hassell said, suggesting Ribbentrop was hard to get along with. When Göring said he thought Hitler's sixteen points quite reasonable, Hassell told him Henderson believed they now were invalid. Göring got excited at that. Ignorant of Hitler's declaration that the offer had expired at midnight, he asked why Henderson would think such a thing. The proposal would be invalid only if the Poles failed to show up, Göring said. When Hassell agreed to tell Henderson the offer remained valid until a representative came, Göring said, "Yes, but he must come at once."[5]

When Dahlerus arrived at the British embassy at about ten in the morning, he found Henderson dejected, viewing everything as hopeless. After Dahlerus insisted that the Poles send a negotiator, Henderson arranged for him to see Lipski, and the Swede and Ogilvie-Forbes went off to the Polish embassy. They found the main hall filled with packing cases. Evacuation was in the air. The staff was packing everything. Much of the furniture had apparently been moved out already. Lipski was pale and nervous. When Lipski asked Dahlerus to read him the proposal, he listened but finally said he could not understand it. When Ogilvie-Forbes wrote down the main points and handed the paper to him, Lipski's fingers trembled. The ambassador looked at the document for a minute and said he could not read it. He then sent Dahlerus off with a secretary to dictate the note to her.

While they were alone, Lipski confided o Ogilvie-Forbes that he was not interested in whatever notes or proposal the Germans might offer. He had been in Berlin for more than five years and understood Germany well. He said he and his compatriots in Warsaw were convinced that if Hitler invaded Poland, the German people would rise up. Hitler would be overthrown, and a victorious Polish army would march into Berlin, he declared. It was a shocking view and a disastrous one as well. The question was whether Lipski was right when he said the leaders in Warsaw shared it.[6]

Whether they did or not, Warsaw telegraphed Lipski shortly after noon, ordering him to get a meeting with Ribbentrop and say Britain had forwarded the proposals to Warsaw, where they were being considered "in a favorable spirit." The telegram, which the Germans had intercepted, also stated, "Do not get into any factual discussions." If the Germans made any proposals, he was to tell them he had no authority to discuss them—he merely was a messenger, waiting for orders from Warsaw.[7]

Despite his reluctance, Lipski called the German foreign ministry asking for an audience with the führer, but having read the intercept, Hitler refused to see the ambassador.[8] He told his generals the Poles were merely trying to delay matters. Ribbentrop had convinced him there was no point in any more diplomacy. Furious, Göring unleashed to those around him his total disdain of Ribbentrop.[9]

Hell-bent on invasion and apparently aware that Lipski would have no power to negotiate, Ribbentrop told his staff he, too, would not see the man. Weizsäcker recommended that he be seen nevertheless. Ribbentrop continued to refuse, and in a heated session in the Reich Chancellery, Weizsäcker urged him again to see Lipski. Their confrontation grew so loud people around began to take note. At one point, Weizsäcker threatened to resign, and at another, he told Ribbentrop he would be "a swine" if he did not tell the foreign minister what he thought. Finally, Ribbentrop relented, and Weizsäcker scheduled the Polish diplomat for a meeting late that afternoon.[10]

Meanwhile, Dahlerus conceived the idea that perhaps Göring and Henderson, who would represent both Britain and Poland at their meeting, could work out a solution to the crisis. Hitler had not forgotten that it was a similar discussion between the two countries that had resulted in the dismemberment of Czechoslovakia, so he approved. Göring invited the ambassador to tea.

Henderson, who brought Ogilvie-Forbes with him, seemed guarded about Göring's proposal and said only that he would forward it to London. The meeting went nowhere. Having nothing more to offer, Göring launched a lamentation against the Poles' delay and an anthem for friendship with England. The reichsmarschall seemed to ignore the fact he had contributed to the Poles' fear of enduring the fate of Hácha, having helped Hitler bully the old man by threatening to bomb Prague. The meeting had gone on for nearly two hours when Göring was called out to take a phone call. Göring returned to the room to say Lipski was on his way to see Ribbentrop, and he seemed vastly relieved. With that, Henderson and Ogilvie-Forbes returned to the British embassy, where the staff was burning all the documents.[11]

At six thirty, Lipski presented himself at the foreign ministry and read to Ribbentrop the portion of the telegram that said Warsaw was "favorably considering" Britain's suggestion that they negotiate. Lipski said they would respond to the sixteen-point proposal in the next few hours.[12]

"Have you authority to negotiate with us now on the German proposals?" asked Ribbentrop, knowing what Lipski's response would be.

"No," the ambassador said.

"Well then, there is no point in our continuing this conversation," Ribbentrop declared, ending the meeting.[13] When Lipski returned to his embassy and picked up the phone to report the event to Warsaw, he found all the embassy's lines were dead.[14]

"Since the evening of August 30 they have obviously been firmly resolved to go to war whatever happens," Weizsäcker wrote in a note to himself. "I suspect," he added, "that it was Ribbentrop's advice which turned the scales." Despondent, Weizsäcker called Göring, telling him this would be the end of Germany.

With that, Göring went to Hitler and urged him to call off the invasion and negotiate. Hitler refused, shouting him down. Göring begged him a second time, and again Hitler shouted him down. A third time, Göring pled and was once again shouted down.[15]

Inside the headquarters of the high command, just outside the offices of the Abwehr, Canaris encountered a secret ally, Hans Bernd Gisevius, who had worked with him in the plot to overthrow Hitler at Munich. Canaris had just come from a meeting of senior officers and was obviously upset. He grabbed Gisevius's arms and stared down at the floor. "Well, what do you say now?" he asked.

Gisevius said nothing, and fighting off tears, the admiral said, "This means the end of Germany."[16]

* * *

That evening, Hitler got the trumped-up excuse he wanted for invading Poland. Heinrich Himmler had senior officers of his SS take thirteen prisoners from a concentration camp, drug them, put them in Polish uniforms, and take them to the outskirts of the border town of Gleiwitz. They then seized a German radio station, where one of Himmler's men who spoke Polish made a broadcast urging all Poles in the town to rise up against Germany. They then made certain all the unconscious convicts were lying facing toward Germany before they shot them and left. Almost immediately, Goebbels's propaganda operators began announcing that the Poles had tried to invade.

Close to midnight, the early editions of the next morning's papers hit the streets. The propaganda ministry had them given away free, and the headlines screamed, "Poland Refuses! Attack about to Begin!"[17]

15

INVASION

T HE MORNING OF SEPTEMBER 1 DAWNED COOL IN Berlin, with a layer of gray clouds hanging over the city.[1]

Off the Westerplatte in Danzig's harbor, the *Schleswig-Holstein* was still sitting at anchor. The battleship was a training vessel for German naval cadets, and at precisely 4:45 a.m., the cadets turned its guns on the complex of Polish military buildings, which included a munitions depot, and opened fire.

Simultaneously, German artillery pieces all along the Polish border began firing as well. From Germany on the west, the state of East Prussia on the north, and German-occupied Slovakia to the south, tanks roared to life and lurched forward, followed by more than a million infantrymen. In all, Germany was unleashing more than 1.6 million men on Poland. Six hundred thousand were coming from East Prussia and northern Germany, and nearly nine hundred thousand were moving in from Slovakia and southern Germany.[2]

Despite the expectations of Lipski and his bosses in Warsaw, the Polish army, which still depended heavily on horses, was ill equipped to stand up to the might of the Wehrmacht. Nevertheless, the Poles waged a valiant defense.

Bombers of the Luftwaffe were wiping out Polish airplanes before they could take off. Other bombers attacked railroad junctions and army mobilization centers. Fighters were strafing highways. Soon, tanks and motorized infantry were encircling Polish army units, cutting them off in the inauguration of Hitler's new *blitzkrieg* or "lightning war."[3] Hitler had launched his war with a flourish.

* * *

That morning, Albert Forster, the Nazi gauleiter of Danzig, proclaimed that Danzig was now part of Germany and had the swastika flag hoisted over all public buildings.[4]

Shortly before ten o'clock, Hitler rode to the Kroll Opera House, where the Reichstag held its infrequent meetings. There he was to give the world his account of the failed peace talks. Loudspeakers had been mounted on the sidewalks along the way to carry Hitler's speech, and as he went along, Nazi marching songs played from them. Except for a thin line of SS troops at the curbside, few people were on the streets, and most seemed to ignore Hitler's motorcade. In fact, the people displayed a marked lack of enthusiasm for the war.[5] As Lipski had predicted, war was not popular among the Germans. But they lacked the spirit and the ability to revolt and respond as he had predicted.

The legislature had moved to the Kroll Opera House after its palace had been burned in 1933. Although some suspected Göring had had a hand in it, he always insisted he was innocent.

The stage insider the opera house where Wagner had been performed had been refitted into a grandiose set for Hitler to perform. In the stage's center, raised above everyone else, sat a dais where Hermann Göring presided as the president of the Reichstag. Down below was a podium where Hitler always spoke. To the sides on the stage were seats for assorted dignitaries. In the front row, set aside from the rest, sat Ribbentrop and Hess and others of the führer's hierarchy.

The wall behind was of gold, and on its lower center was a swastika encircled by a wreath. The pair resembled the sun, and golden rays spread out from them. Over them a giant eagle clutched the wreath in its talons.

As he always did when making a speech, Hitler stood stiffly at attention, the heels of his black boots pressed together.[6] He was not wearing his usual party uniform of brown. Instead, he was dressed in the green uniform of the German army. His voice was husky—some said strained. Some also thought he seemed stunned by what he had done and sounded as if he were tired.[7] As he talked, planes could be heard flying over the city. Every so often, as they usually did, the deputies would interrupt him, jump up, their hands raised, and shout, "Heil!"

"I have put on the uniform of the soldier," he announced. "It will not be taken off until Germany is victorious. If I should fall on the battlefield, Hermann Göring is to be my successor."

Hitler concluded by declaring that "German 'steel' will vanquish." Then he bellowed, "Deutschland—Sieg Heil!" meaning "Germany, hail victory." On cue, as they did at Nazi rallies, the deputies jumped up once more, arms out in salute, and cried "Heil!" and every time Hitler repeated "Sieg," they responded "Heil!" Then they broke into the national anthem: "Deutchland, Deutchland, uber alles" (Germany, Germany, over all).

Giuseppe Verdi could not have done better when he scripted the scene for the victorious march in his opera *Aida*.

* * *

While Hitler had been speaking, Dahlerus had been meeting with Henderson. The two had seen Hitler drive past on his way to the Kroll Opera House, and as they talked, they could hear bits of Hitler's speech from the loudspeakers out on the sidewalk. Dahlerus had come from a meeting with Göring, where the reichsmarschall had given the Swede the party line about the invasion. It had been caused by the Poles, he charged. Despite his assertions, Göring realized the only way to keep the west from declaring war on Germany was to find a way to keep up the peace talks. In that light, he and Dahlerus had agreed the only way to prevent a world war was to persuade Hitler to allow Göring to meet with the British. That would require Henderson's support, and the ambassador seemed to think it all hopeless. Bitterly, he lambasted Hitler and Ribbentrop, asserting that they had brought Europe to the brink of war.

About an hour after arriving at the Kroll, Hitler's motorcade returned to the chancellery. Göring returned with him and persuaded Hitler to try the plan he and Dahlerus had come up with. He soon tracked down the Swede at the embassy and told him to come up the street to the chancellery immediately. Hitler wanted to see him.

The Wilhelmstrasse now was filled with people, and the area in front of the chancellery was blocked off, so Göring sent two Luftwaffe officers to escort Dahlerus through the barricade. Inside the chancellery, he found all the senior officers of the Reich milling about. As he was escorted through, Dahlerus passed Hess and Himmler. When Göring appeared, he told Dahlerus that Hitler had made him second-in-command. That, he said, would give him more authority to bring about a peaceful solution. Dahlerus told the reichsmarschall that he saw little hope of preventing a war. Göring then went off to see Hitler, came back, and took Dahlerus into another room, where he found the führer. He was alone, and to the Swede, he seemed nervous, like he was trying to hide the fact that he was disturbed. He received Dahlerus graciously but then unnerved the Swede by coming up close and staring into his eyes as he spoke. Hitler's breath was so bad Dahlerus wanted to back away. Hitler provided every argument he could to justify the invasion. Just as Henderson had said, Hitler declared it was hopeless trying to reach an agreement. When Göring tried to say something, Hitler cut him off, explaining that he was determined to vanquish the Poles and annihilate their nation. If Britain wanted to talk, he said, he would be happy to meet the country halfway, adding, "But if the British don't understand that it is in their own interests to keep out of a fight with me, they will live to repent their folly."

Getting increasingly worked up, Hitler began waving his arms and shouting into Dahlerus's face. "If England wants to fight for a year, I shall fight for a year. If England wants to fight two years, I shall fight two years." At that, he paused and then waved his arms wildly, and his voice rose to a shrill scream as he said, "If England wants to fight for three years, I shall fight for three years!" Hitler's body began moving from side to side in concert with his arms. Then, after another pause, he shouted at the top of his voice, "And if necessary, I can fight for ten years!" Hitler balled up his fist, and bending, he stretched his arm almost to the floor. Dahlerus stood embarrassed. Göring seemed so embarrassed, too, that he had turned his back on the scene.

Dahlerus left convinced there was no hope if the fate of Europe lay in the hands of a madman like Hitler. For his part, Göring was, as Dahlerus described it, "nervous and distraught."[8] Soon afterward, the French government announced that it was ordering general mobilization effective the next morning.[9]

* * *

During the past several days, Benito Mussolini had been making his own preparations for the moment Hitler launched his invasion. Since the Italian people were anti-German and against any war and Italy did not have the resources to join in, Mussolini had been taking steps to convince the people that he had been prepared to fight too. Rome had staged blackouts, cafés had been ordered to close at night, and soldiers were called to arms, all to make him look like the warrior he wanted to be. That had unnerved the British and French, who believed Mussolini was about to attack them, and on the night of August 31, Britain had cut its telephone lines to Italy.

The next day, with the invasion well underway, Mussolini called Attolico, asking him to get Hitler to send a telegram releasing him from his obligation to join forces with Germany. Hitler responded promptly, assuring Il Duce that Germany could handle Poland alone. To prove that he was not walking away from Italy's obligation, Mussolini had the telegram broadcast to the Italian people.[10]

The French pressed Italy to offer again to mediate the issue, but the British were skeptical of the idea, and Mussolini and Ciano were more so. Knowing how determined Hitler was to wipe out Poland, Mussolini saw no point in trying.[11] Hitler grew less interested in a settlement when he met with his "cabinet" of top underlings at six in the evening, and the army reported that it was sweeping aside Polish resistance and advancing on all fronts.[12]

In London, Neville Chamberlain told the House of Commons that Britain was not backing down, saying, "The time has come when action rather than speech is required." He announced that he would ask the Commons to amend the conscription act to make all fit men between the ages of eighteen and forty-one liable for the draft. The blame for this war, he declared, "lies on the shoulders of one man, the German chancellor, who has not hesitated to plunge the world into misery in order to serve his own senseless ambitions."[13]

Early that evening, the French and British ambassadors asked to meet with Ribbentrop together, but he refused, insisting that they come separately.[14] At nine thirty that night, Henderson arrived at the foreign ministry and handed Ribbentrop a note from London. Unless Germany stopped firing and prepared to withdraw from Poland, it said, "His Majesty's Government will without hesitation fulfill its obligations to Poland."[15] Ribbentrop acted as if he did not understand English, and Schmidt translated the note for him.[16] The foreign minister insisted to Henderson that it was the Poles who had started the war, claiming they had mobilized first and invaded Germany first.[17]

At ten o'clock, Coulondre was ushered in. He delivered an identical message, and in return, Ribbentrop gave him an identical speech.[18]

* * *

That night at the Esplanade Hotel, where Dahlerus usually stayed, some of the staff—aware that he knew Göring—came to him asking whether he thought the war might be avoided. "It was extraordinary to note that not one of all these people," Dahlerus wrote later, "showed hatred of Poland. All of them behaved like timid animals before an approaching danger."[19]

16

ULTIMATUM

THE FOLLOWING MORNING, SATURDAY, SEPTEMBER 2, THE FRENCH again pressed Mussolini to offer mediation, and Attolico appeared at the foreign ministry and delivered to Weizsäcker a proposal that Germany and the others meet. Weizsäcker took the offer to Hitler himself, cutting out Ribbentrop so that the foreign minister could not influence the führer's decision.[1] As a result, Hitler was open to the idea, and when Attolico reported this to Rome, Ciano was surprised. But then the British began insisting that before they held any meeting, Hitler had to withdraw all his troops from Poland. Knowing that Hitler would never approve that condition, Ciano dropped the matter, and with that, he noted sadly that all hopes for peace were gone.[2]

That afternoon, near a railroad crossing in northwestern Poland, a German lieutenant named Heinrich von Weizsäcker was killed leading his platoon. He was a son of Ernst von Weizsäcker and one of the first casualties of the war. His brother, Richard, who was in the same regiment, watched over his body through much of the night.[3] Over the next six years, more than four million German soldiers, sailors, and airmen would follow Heinrich.

* * *

That evening, the British embassy asked the German foreign office for an audience with Henderson on the following day, Sunday, September 3, at nine in the morning. Schmidt had overslept and was emerging from a cab when he saw Henderson ascending the front steps of the foreign ministry. Ducking in a side entrance, Schmidt hurried to Ribbentrop's office just in time to receive the ambassador. Ribbentrop was next door in the chancellery with Hitler, waiting to see what Henderson might have come to say.

The ambassador was obviously distressed as he read to Schmidt a note to the German government from London. Henderson handed Schmidt the document and departed, and the interpreter went to Hitler's study in the New Chancellery. The anteroom was so filled with Nazi leaders Schmidt had trouble getting past.

When he entered the study, Hitler was sitting at his desk, and Ribbentrop was standing by the window looking out at the chancellery garden. Both looked at him with expectation. Schmidt stood in front of Hitler's desk and began to interpret the note slowly. "More than twenty-four hours have elapsed since an immediate reply was requested to the warning of September 1, and since then the attacks on Poland have been intensified," he read. The note went on to announce that if the British government did not receive "satisfactory assurances" by eleven in the morning that Germany was halting its attack and withdrawing its forces from Poland, "from that time a state of war will exist between Great Britain and Germany."

Hitler did not move. He just sat in silence. Finally, he turned to Ribbentrop and glared angrily at the man who had encouraged him into this mess. "What now?" he said coldly.[4]

Ribbentrop said nothing and soon left. Schmidt took his leave as well. Hitler continued sitting, slumped in his chair, trying to comprehend what had happened.

Outside in the anteroom, Schmidt gave everyone the news. The room fell silent. Goebbels stood in a corner looking despondent. Göring turned to Schmidt and broke the silence. "If we lose this war, then God have mercy on us!"[5]

Heinrich Hoffmann, who had been waiting with the others, went in. Hitler looked over from his chair, saying bitterly, "And for this, my friend, we have to thank those fools, the so-called experts of the foreign office." Hoffmann knew Hitler was talking not about the diplomats but about Ribbentrop.[6]

Hitler might have blamed Ribbentrop or the foreign office, but the true responsibility for this worldwide disaster lay solely on him. As Göring had once told Henderson, "When a decision has to be taken, none of us count more than the stones on which we are standing. It is the führer alone who decides."[7]

An hour or so after Henderson had delivered the ultimatum, Erich Raeder, who commanded the navy, was summoned to the study, where he found a number of men gathered, including Hitler's deputy, Rudolf Hess.

Contrary to his hopes, Hitler told Raeder, Britain had delivered an ultimatum and they were going to war. Hitler was so embarrassed he could not hide it. "It was an expression of embarrassment such as I had never noticed on Hitler," Raeder said.[8]

*   *   *

The Polish depot in Danzig held out for a week, despite barrages from the battleship and attacks from Stuka dive-bombers and infantry. The Stukas were fitted with whistles that caused them to scream as they dived, creating panic on the ground below. Bombed and battered, Warsaw would fall September 27. The Germans would take all of Poland by October 6.

On September 17, the Russian army, taking advantage of the secret deal Stalin and Hitler had made, would march in from the east, and Poland would be divided once again by Germany and Russia. In the process, the Soviets would secretly massacre much of Poland's officer corps in the Katyn Forest.

In the Western Hemisphere, history was beginning to repeat itself. Time after time Göring had warned Hitler that if Germany went to war with England, the United States would do as it had in World War I and enter the war on Britain's side. But Hitler had insisted that would never happen.[9]

It already was being discussed. On August 30, at the White House, two days before the invasion of Poland, Franklin Roosevelt had suggested to Lord Lothian, the British ambassador, that the United States and other American nations declare the western Atlantic out-of-bounds to any belligerent warships. Only weeks after the start of the war, the nations of the Americas did that, offering protection to British convoys from attack everywhere west of Iceland.[10]

In hindsight, Poland could have allowed Lipski the power to negotiate. Even had he agreed to Hitler's sixteen-point offer and allowed the Germans a corridor through the Polish Corridor and given Germany Danzig, Hitler would have been back a year of two later demanding more. If the British had backed off their support of Poland, the Poles never would have backed down.

The Germans had gambled wrong. They had totally misread Poland and the British and the French. And it was all because of the Champagne Salesman.

17

FINIS

GERMANY LOST THE WAR IN THE SPRING OF 1945. Hitler killed himself in his bunker beneath the New Reich Chancellery that he had built with such personal attention. The Allies also were battling the Japanese in the Pacific, and in August, the Americans ended that war by dropping atom bombs on two Japanese cities. Oddly enough, considering Göring's nickname, the code word for one of those bombs was Fat Man.

That November, a tribunal composed of American, French, British, and Russian judges convened in Nuremberg to try some of the top German leaders for war crimes, including Göring and Ribbentrop.

Göring's American guards liked him.[1] It was a bit ironic that he was on trial since he had tried so assiduously to persuade Hitler to stay out of war. One of the Americans appointed to prosecute him said privately he thought the reichsmarschall should never have been charged.[2]

When the tribunal sentenced him and ten others to be hanged, Fat Boy avoided the gallows by taking a cyanide capsule the night before his execution. Göring claimed in a letter that he left for the commander of the prison that he had smuggled in three such capsules: one for the guards to find, another hidden on his person, and the third in a jar of skin cream.[3] For years, there were rumors that a guard had slipped the pill to him, and indeed, decades later, a former guard made the admission of his involvement. His story might have been true, and Göring's note merely an attempt to protect that soldier.[4]

The day before the invasion of Poland, Weizsäcker had warned Göring that if war came, Germany's leaders would go to the gallows, and he declared that Ribbentrop would be the first.[5] At two in the morning on October 16, 1946, the executions began, and the first to be hanged was the Champagne Salesman.

NOTES

1. Kaiser Wilhelm's Legacy

1. For the causes of World War I, see A. J. P. Taylor, *The Struggle for Mastery in Europe, 1848–1918* (Oxford: Clarendon Press, 1954).

2. The Eloquent Artist

1. Herbert Döhring, Karl Krause, and Anna Plaim, *Living with Hitler: Accounts of Hitler's Household Staff* (Barnsley, UK: Greenhill Books, 2018), 27.

2. Otto Dietrich, *The Hitler I Knew: The Memoirs of the Third Reich's Press Chief* (New York: Skyhorse, 2010), 16, 198; Döhring, Krause, and Plaim, *Living with Hitler*, 27.

3. August Kubizek, *Young Hitler: The Story of Our Friendship* (Maidstone, UK: Mann, 1973), 8.

4. D. Jablow Hershman and Julian Lieb, *A Brotherhood of Tyrants: Manic Depression and Absolute Power* (Amherst: Prometheus Books, 1994).

5. Joachim von Ribbentrop, *The Ribbentrop Memoirs* (London: Weidenfeld and Nicolson, 1954), 30.

6. Kubizek, *Young Hitler*, 11.

7. Kubizek, 11–12.

8. In a memo on December 3, 1943, a member of the US Office of Strategic Services (OSS), the forerunner of the Central Intelligence Agency, assessed Hitler. The memo was classified secret. Much of the member's assessment was based on the account of one of Hitler's earliest friends, Dr. Ernst "Putzi" Hanfstaengl, who had been interned by the British and, after the intercession of an old friend, Franklin Roosevelt, became a consultant to the US government. The memo refers to Hanfstaengl by a code name, "Dr. Sedgwick," though Sedgwick was actually his middle name.

9. Dietrich, *Hitler I Knew*, 10.

10. Ernst Hanfstaengl, *Hitler: The Missing Years* (London: Eyre & Spottiswoode, 1957), 271–289.

11. OSS memo.

12. Dietrich, *Hitler I Knew*, 36.

13. Dietrich, 198.

14. Kubizek, *Young Hitler*, 15.

15. Kurt Krueger, *I Was Hitler's Doctor* (New York: Biltmore, 1943), 81.

16. Kubizek, *Young Hitler*, 3–34.

17. Krueger, *I Was Hitler's Doctor*, 60.

18. Leonard Mosley, *On Borrowed Time: How World War II Began* (New York: Random House, 1969), 7–8.

19. After the takeover, the Nazis imprisoned Schuschnigg, holding him for seven years, until he was freed by American troops at the end of World War II.

20. All the events leading up to World War II are best summed up in A. J. P. Taylor, *The Origins of the Second World War* (New York: Atheneum, 1962).

21. Wilhelm Keitel, *The Memoirs of Field Marshal Keitel* (New York: Stein and Day, 1966), 62; Dietrich, *Hitler I Knew*, 31.

22. Paul Schmidt, *Hitler's Interpreter* (New York: Macmillan, 1951).

23. Winston S. Churchill, *The Gathering Storm* (Boston: Houghton Mifflin, 1948), 327.

3. The Champagne Salesman

1. Michael Bloch, *Ribbentrop* (New York: Crown, 1992), 6–8; Joachim von Ribbentrop, *The Ribbentrop Memoirs* (London: Weidenfeld and Nicolson, 1954), 9–12.

2. Ribbentrop, *Ribbentrop Memoirs*, 15.

3. Bloch, *Ribbentrop*, 12–14; Albert Speer, *Spandau: The Secret Diaries* (New York: Macmillan, 1976), 142.

4. Speer, *Spandau*, 142.

5. Bloch, 17–18.

6. For the whole story of the negotiations, see Bloch, 28–33.

7. Bloch, 14.

8. Paul Schwarz, *This Man Ribbentrop, His Life and Times* (New York: Messner, 1943), 36.

9. Bloch, *Ribbentrop*, 67.

10. Bloch, 113.

11. John Weitz, *Hitler's Diplomat: The Life and Times of Joachim von Ribbentrop* (New York: Ticknor and Fields, 1992), 119.

12. Winston S. Churchill, *The Gathering Storm* (Boston: Houghton Mifflin, 1948), 223.

13. Bloch, *Ribbentrop*, 98.

14. G. M. Gilbert, *Nuremberg Diary* (New York: Farrar, Straus, 1947), 13.

4. Fat Boy's Swedish Friend

1. Ernst von Weizsäcker, *Memoirs* (Chicago: Regnery, 1951), 156.

2. John Weitz, *Hitler's Diplomat: The Life and Times of Joachim von Ribbentrop* (New York: Ticknor and Fields, 1992), 185.

3. Michael Bloch, *Ribbentrop* (New York: Crown, 1992), 43–44.

4. Albert Speer, *Inside the Third Reich* (New York: Macmillan, 1970), 84–85.

5. *Documents of German Foreign Policy* (*DGFP*), series D, vol. 5 (Washington, DC: US Government Printing Office, 1949), 157.

6. *The Polish White Book: Official Documents concerning Polish-German and Polish-Soviet Relations 1933-1939* (London: Hutchinson, 1940), 47–48.

7. Nevile Henderson, *Failure of a Mission: Berlin 1937-1939* (New York: Putnam, 1940), 190, 233; Leonard Mosley, *On Borrowed Time: How World War II Began* (New York: Random House, 1969), 263.

8. *Polish White Book*, 49.

9. *DGFP*, 156.

10. Weitz, *Hitler's Diplomat*, 195–96.

11. *Polish White Book*, 56.

12. Leonard Mosley, *The Reich Marshal: A Biography of Hermann Goering* (Garden City, NY: Doubleday, 1974), 229–31.

13. *Polish White Book*, 69–70.

14. Hans Bernd Gisevius, *To the Bitter End* (Boston: Houghton Mifflin, 1947), 363.

15. Ernst von Weizsäcker, *Memoirs* (Chicago: Regnery, 1951), 180.

16. Wilhelm Keitel, *The Memoirs of Field Marshal Keitel* (New York: Stein and Day, 1966), 84.

17. For more on Dodd's service in Berlin, see Erik Larson, *In the Garden of Beasts: Love, Terror, and an American Family in Hitler's Berlin* (New York: Crown, 2011).

18. Axton, Matilda F., et al., eds. "The Ambassador in France (Bullitt) to the Secretary of State," *Foreign Relations of US Diplomatic Papers (USDP)*, vol. 1, document 110 (Washington, DC: US Government Printing Office, 1956).

19. Axton et al., eds., "President Roosevelt to the German Chancellor (Hitler)," *USDP*, document 120; Mosley, *On Borrowed Time*, 216–18. The two countries held Syria and Palestine as protectorates as a result of the peace treaty the Allies had signed with Turkey at the end of World War I.

20. Keitel, *The Memoirs of Field Marshal Keitel*, 85–86.

21. Keitel, 84–85.

22. Speer, *Inside the Third Reich*, 195.

23. Paul Schwarz, *This Man Ribbentrop His Life and Times* (New York: Messner, 1943), 46–48.

24. US Department of State, Special Interrogation Mission to Germany, 1945–1946, interrogation of Herman Göring, National Archives.

25. Mosley, *On Borrowed Time*, 281.

26. Mosley, *Reich Marshal*, 100–104, 214.

27. Mosley, 189, 235.

28. Speer, *Inside the Third Reich*, 43–44.

29. G. M. Gilbert, *Nuremberg Diary* (New York: Farrar, Straus, 1947), 435.

30. Mosley, *Reich Marshal*, 215–16.

31. Mosley, 237.

32. Mosley, 230–31.

33. Birger Dahlerus, *The Last Attempt* (London: Hutchinson, 1947), 19.

34. Dahlerus, 13–16.

35. Dahlerus, 23–27.

36. Dahlerus, 29–31.

37. Dahlerus, 44–48.

38. Mosley, *On Borrowed Time*, 242–44.

39. Speer, *Inside the Third Reich*, 193–94.

40. Mosley, *Reich Marshal*, 237–38.

41. Mosley, *On Borrowed Time*, 366–67; Gilbert, *Nuremberg Diary*, 230.

5. "Close Your Hearts to Pity!"

1. Notes of the conference by Halder, *Documents of German Foreign Policy (DGFP)*, series D, vol. 7 (Washington, DC: US Government Printing Office, 1949), 555.

2. Wilhelm Keitel, *The Memoirs of Field Marshal Keitel* (New York: Stein and Day, 1966), 87.

3. Walter Görlitz, *History of the German General Staff, 1657–1945* (New York: Praeger, 1953), 351.

4. Charles Messenger, *The Last Prussian: A Biography of Field Marshal Gerd von Rundstedt, 1875–1953* (London: Brassey's, 1991), 84.

5. Ernst von Weizsäcker, *Memoirs* (Chicago: Regnery, 1951), 135.

6. Erich von Manstein, *Lost Victories* (Novato, CA: Presidio, 1982), 28.

7. Quotes of Hitler's speech in this chapter come from Franz Halder, *The Halder War Diary, 1939–1942* (Novato, CA: Presidio, 1988), 28–32; for Halder's notes of the meeting, see *DGFP*, 557–59.

8. Manstein, *Lost Victories*, 30–31.

9. Office of United States Chief of Counsel for Prosecution of Axis Criminality, *Nazi Conspiracy and Aggression*, supplement B (Washington, DC: US Government Printing Office, 1948), 1103–4.

6. A Performance of Bombast and Threats

1. For more on Hitler's dinner routines, see Otto Dietrich, *The Hitler I Knew: The Memoirs of the Third Reich's Press Chief* (New York: Skyhorse, 2010), 168–74.

2. Dietrich, 119.

3. Birger Dahlerus, *The Last Attempt* (London: Hutchinson, 1947), 49.

4. *Documents of German Foreign Policy* (*DGFP*), series D, vol. 7 (Washington, DC: US Government Printing Office, 1949), 246–47.

5. Quotes for this meeting are taken from Ernst von Weizsäcker, *Memoirs* (Chicago: Regnery, 1951), 202–4; Nevile Henderson, *Failure of a Mission: Berlin 1937–1939* (New York: Putnam, 1940), 268–70; Great Britain Foreign Office, *The British War Blue Book* (New York: Farrar and Rinehart, 1939), 127–30; *DGFP*, 210–19.

6. Galeazzo Ciano, *The Ciano Diaries, 1939–1943* (New York: Doubleday, 1946), 582.

7. Galeazzo, *Ciano Diaries*, 127.

8. *DGFP*, 220–21; Joachim von Ribbentrop, *The Ribbentrop Memoirs* (London: Weidenfeld and Nicolson, 1954), 113.

9. Nicolaus von Below, *At Hitler's Side: The Memoirs of Hitler's Luftwaffe Adjutant, 1937–1945* (Mechanicsburg, PA: Stackpole Books, 1980), 27–28.

7. "A Second Bismarck"

1. Ernst von Weizsäcker, *Memoirs* (Chicago: Regnery, 1951), 204; *Documents of German Foreign Policy* (*DGFP*) series D, vol. 7 (Washington, DC: US Government Printing Office, 1949), 240–43.

2. Otto Dietrich, *The Hitler I Knew: The Memoirs of the Third Reich's Press Chief* (New York: Skyhorse, 2010), 226.

3. Joachim von Ribbentrop, *The Ribbentrop Memoirs* (London: Weidenfeld and Nicolson, 1954), 115; Hans Baur, *Hitler at My Side* (Houston: Eichler, 1986), 118.

4. Paul Schmidt, *Hitler's Interpreter* (New York: Macmillan, 1951), 138–39.

5. Schmidt, *Hitler's Interpreter*, 188; US War Department, *Handbook on German Military Forces* (Washington, DC: US Government Publishing Office, 1945), chapter 10.

6. Birger Dahlerus, *The Last Attempt* (London: Hutchinson, 1947), 50–51.

7. Weather record at Tempelhof Airport, August 24, 1939.

8. Associated Press dispatch, August 24, 1939; Associated Press photos.

9. Albert Speer, *Inside the Third Reich* (New York: Macmillan, 1970) 196.

10. Speer, *Inside the Third Reich*, 87–94.

11. Quotes from the meeting are from Heinrich Hoffmann, *Hitler Was My Friend* (Barnsley, UK: Frontline Books, 2011), 112; see also Michael Bloch, *Ribbentrop* (New York: Crown, 1992), 250; Hans Bernd Gisevius, *To the Bitter End* (Boston: Houghton Mifflin, 1947), 365–66; Weizsäcker, *Memoirs*, 204–5; Dahlerus, *Last Attempt*, 51–53.

8. Et Tu, Bruté?

1. Weather record at Tempelhof Airport, August 25, 1939.

2. Galeazzo Ciano, *The Ciano Diaries, 1939–1943* (New York: Doubleday, 1946), 128; *Documents of German Foreign Policy* (*DGFP*), series D, vol. 7 (Washington, DC: US Government Printing Office, 1949), 278.

3. Ciano, *Ciano Diaries*, 128; *DGFP*, 278.

4. *DGFP*, 281–83.

5. Ciano, *Ciano Diaries*, 128.

6. Hans Bernd Gisevius, *To the Bitter End* (Boston: Houghton Mifflin, 1947), 366–67.

7. Great Britain Foreign Office, *The British War Blue Book* (New York: Farrar and Rinehart, 1939), 138–53.

8. Associated Press dispatch, August 25, 1939.

9. *DGFP*, 281–83.

10. Paul Schmidt, *Hitler's Interpreter* (New York: Macmillan, 1951), 142; *DGFP*, 297–98.

11. Franz Halder, *The Halder War Diary, 1939–1942* (Novato, CA: Presidio, 1988), 34.

12. Joachim von Ribbentrop, *The Ribbentrop Memoirs* (London: Weidenfeld and Nicolson, 1954), 116.

13. Schmidt, *Hitler's Interpreter*, 143; Nevile Henderson, *Failure of a Mission: Berlin 1937–1939* (New York: Putnam, 1940), 272.

14. Halder, *Halder War Diary*, 34.

15. *New York Times*, January 13, 1939; Albert Speer, *Inside the Third Reich* (New York: Macmillan, 1970), 136. For other details on the New Chancellery, see Steven Lehrer, *The Reich Chancellery and Führerbunker Complex: An Illustrated History of the Seat of the Nazi Regime* (Jefferson, NC: McFarland, 2006).

16. Schmidt, *Hitler's Interpreter*, 142–43; DGFP, 279–81; Great Britain Foreign Office, *The British War Blue Book*, 155–59; Henderson, *Failure of a Mission*, 272.

17. *Documents of British Foreign Policy* (*DBFP*), series 3 (London: Her Majesty's Stationery Office, 1954), 257.

18. *DBFP*, 257–59.

19. Ciano, *Ciano Diaries*, 128; *DGFP*, 281.

20. Schmidt, *Hitler's Interpreter*, 143–44; *Diplomatic Documents of Italy*, series 8, vol. 13, 168–69.

21. Halder, *Halder War Diary*, 34.

22. Ernst von Weizsäcker, *Memoirs* (Chicago: Regnery, 1951), 206.

23. Schmidt, *Hitler's Interpreter*, 143.

24. Schmidt, 144–45; *The French Yellow Book*, diplomatic documents, 1938–39, no. 242 (London: Hutchinson, 1940).

25. Ciano, *Ciano Diaries*, 128.

26. Ribbentrop, *Ribbentrop Memoirs*, 116–17; Office of United States Chief of Counsel for Prosecution of Axis Criminality, *Nazi Conspiracy and Aggression* (Washington, DC: US Government Printing Office, 1948), 535–36, 1223; *Trial of the Major War Criminals before the International Military Tribunal (TMWC)*, vol. 10 (Nuremburg, Germany: Secretariat of the Tribunal, 1947), 270; *DGFP*, 285–286.

27. Schmidt, *Hitler's Interpreter*, 145–46.

28. Ciano, *Ciano Diaries*, 127; *DBFP*, 185–86, 220.

29. Wilhelm Keitel, *The Memoirs of Field Marshal Keitel* (New York: Stein and Day, 1966), 88–90; Schmidt, *Hitler's Interpreter*, 146–47.

30. Walter Warlimont, *Inside Hitler's Headquarters, 1939–45* (New York: Praeger, 1964), 27.

31. Gisevius's testimony, *TMWC*, vol. 12, 224.

32. Erich von Manstein, *Lost Victories* (Novato, CA: Presidio, 1982), 32.

33. Halder, *Halder War Diary*, 34; Fedor von Bock, *The War Diary, 1939–1945* (Atglen, PA: Schiffer, 1996), 36–37; Charles Messenger, *The Last Prussian: A Biography of Field Marshal Gerd von Rundstedt, 1875–1953* (London: Brassey's, 1991), 86–87; Manstein, *Lost Victories*, 31–32.

34. Halder, *Halder War Diary*, 34; Von Bock, *War Diary*, 36–37; Messenger, *Last Prussian*, 86–87; Manstein, *Lost Victories*, 31–32.

35. *TMWC*, vol. 10, 366.

36. *TMWC*, vol. 9, 596.

37. *DGFP*, 289.

38. Ribbentrop, *Ribbentrop Memoirs*, 117; Warlimont, *Inside Hitler's Headquarters*, 27.

39. Warlimont, *Inside Hitler's Headquarters*, 27.

40. Keitel, *The Memoirs of Field Marshal Keitel*, 89–90; Warlimont, *Inside Hitler's Headquarters*, 27; *DGFP*, 561.

41. *DBFP*, 239.

42. *DBFP*, 242; *TMWC*, vol. 9, 461; Birger Dahlerus, *The Last Attempt* (London: Hutchinson, 1947), 52–53.

9. "It's Enough to Kill a Bull"

1. Galeazzo Ciano, *The Ciano Diaries, 1939–1943* (New York: Doubleday, 1946), 129.

2. *Documents of German Foreign Policy (DGFP)*, series D, vol. 7 (Washington, DC: US Government Printing Office, 1949), 309–10, 314.

3. *DGFP*, 309–10, 314; Wilhelm Keitel, *The Memoirs of Field Marshal Keitel* (New York: Stein and Day, 1966), 90; Paul Schmidt, *Hitler's Interpreter* (New York: Macmillan, 1951), 147. For the sentiments of the Italian diplomats and the royals, including the king, see August entries in Ciano's diary.

4. Franz Halder, *The Halder War Diary, 1939–1942* (Novato, CA: Presidio, 1988), 35.

5. *DGFP*, 313–14.
6. *DGFP*, 313–14.
7. Ciano, *Ciano Diaries*, 129.
8. *DGFP*, 332.
9. *DGFP*, 330–31; *The French Yellow Book*, diplomatic documents, 1938–39, nos. 261 and 262 (London: Hutchinson, 1940).
10. *DGFP*, 330–31; *French Yellow Book*, nos. 261 and 262.
11. *DGFP*, 330–31; *French Yellow Book*, nos. 261 and 262.
12. *DGFP*, 323.
13. *DGFP*, 562.
14. Speer, *Inside the Third Reich* (New York:Macmillan, 1970), 197.
15. Schmidt, *Hitler's Interpreter*, 147; *DGFP*, 346–47.
16. Schmidt, 147; *DGFP*, 346–47.
17. Birger Dahlerus, *The Last Attempt* (London: Hutchinson, 1947), 58–69.
18. Dahlerus, *Last Attempt*, 58–69.
19. Dahlerus, *Last Attempt*, 58–69; *Trial of the Major War Criminals before the International Military Tribunal*, vol. 9 (Nuremburg, Germany: Secretariat of the Tribunal, 1947), 465–66; *Documents of British Foreign Policy*, series 3 (London: Her Majesty's Stationery Office, 1954), 283–86.

10. The Speech That Fell Flat

1. Galeazzo Ciano, *The Ciano Diaries, 1939–1943* (New York: Doubleday, 1946), 130–31; *Documents of British Foreign Policy* (DBFP), series 3 (London: Her Majesty's Stationery Office, 1954), 299, 302.
2. Michael Bloch, *Ribbentrop* (New York: Crown, 1992), 254.
3. Bloch, *Ribbentrop*, 254; Ernst von Weizsäcker, *Memoirs* (Chicago: Regnery, 1951), 208.
4. Ciano, *Ciano Diaries*, 131.
5. *Documents of German Foreign Policy* (DGFP), series D, vol. 7 (Washington, DC: US Government Printing Office, 1949), 564.
6. *DGFP*, 356–60.
7. Wilhelm Keitel, *The Memoirs of Field Marshal Keitel* (New York: Stein and Day, 1966), 91; *DGFP*, 356–60; *The French Yellow Book*, diplomatic documents, 1938–39, no. 267 (London: Hutchinson, 1940).
8. Associated Press dispatch, August 28, 1939.
9. Associated Press wire photo, August 28, 1939.
10. *DGFP*, 563–64.
11. *DGFP*, 562–64.
12. *DGFP*, 562–64; Associated Press dispatches from Berlin, August 27, 1939; Weizsäcker, *Memoirs*, 208; Ulrich von Hassell, *The Ulrich von Hassell Diaries, 1938–1944: The Story of Forces against Hitler inside Germany* (Westport, CT: Greenwood, 2011), 43.
13. Birger Dahlerus, *The Last Attempt* (London: Hutchinson, 1947), 76.
14. *DGFP*, 333–54.
15. *DGFP*, 392.
16. *DGFP*, 361, 368–69.

17. *Trial of the Major War Criminals before the International Military Tribunal*, vol. 9 (Nuremburg, Germany: Secretariat of the Tribunal, 1947), 466–67; *DBFP*, 318–20.

18. Associated Press dispatch, August 28, 1939.

11. Into the Wee Hours

1. Birger Dahlerus, *The Last Attempt* (London: Hutchinson, 1947), 78–81.

2. Dahlerus, *Last Attempt*, 80–81.

3. *Documents of German Foreign Policy* (*DGFP*), series D, vol. 7 (Washington, DC: US Government Printing Office, 1949), 565.

4. Wilhelm Keitel, *The Memoirs of Field Marshal Keitel* (New York: Stein and Day, 1966), 91.

5. Franz Halder, *The Halder War Diary, 1939–1942* (Novato, CA: Presidio, 1988), 39.

6. *DGFP*, 379–80.

7. Nevile Henderson, *Failure of a Mission: Berlin 1937–1939* (New York: Putnam, 1940), 276–77.

8. Henderson, *Failure of a Mission*, 275–80; *Documents of British Foreign Policy* (*DBFP*), series 3 (London: Her Majesty's Stationery Office, 1954), 351–54; *DGFP*, 381–84; Paul Schmidt, *Hitler's Interpreter* (New York: Macmillan, 1951), 148; Joachim von Ribbentrop, *The Ribbentrop Memoirs* (London: Weidenfeld and Nicolson, 1954), 119.

9. Dahlerus, *Last Attempt*, 84.

10. Ernst von Weizsäcker, *Memoirs* (Chicago: Regnery, 1951), 208.

11. *The Polish White Book: Official Documents concerning Polish-German and Polish-Soviet Relations 1933–1939* (London: Hutchinson, 1940), 110–16.

12. A Shouting Match

1. Birger Dahlerus, *The Last Attempt* (London: Hutchinson, 1947), 83.

2. *Documents of German Foreign Policy* (*DGFP*), series D, vol. 7 (Washington, DC: US Government Printing Office, 1949), 360–61.

3. Franz Halder, *The Halder War Diary, 1939–1942* (Novato, CA: Presidio, 1988), 567.

4. *Documents of British Foreign Policy* (*DBFP*), series 3 (London: Her Majesty's Stationery Office, 1954), 339.

5. Paul Schmidt, *Hitler's Interpreter* (New York: Macmillan, 1951), 149; *DGFP*, 407.

6. Quotes from this meeting are from Nevile Henderson, *Failure of a Mission: Berlin 1937–1939* (New York: Putnam, 1940), 277–81; Schmidt, *Hitler's Interpreter*, 149; *Trial of the Major War Criminals before the International Military Tribunal*, vol. 10 (Nuremburg, Germany: Secretariat of the Tribunal, 1947), 368; Joachim von Ribbentrop, *The Ribbentrop Memoirs* (London: Weidenfeld and Nicolson, 1954), 30, 119; *DBFP*, 374–77, 393, 426–27.

7. Henderson, *Failure of a Mission*, 277.

8. Henderson, 280.

9. *DBFP*, 426–27.

10. Galeazzo Ciano, *The Ciano Diaries, 1939–1943* (New York: Doubleday, 1946), 132.

11. Schmidt, *Hitler's Interpreter*, 149.

12. Heinrich Hoffman, *Hitler Was My Friend* (Barnsley, UK: Frontline Books, 2011), 115.
13. *DBFP*, 400–401.
14. Ribbentrop, *Ribbentrop Memoirs*, 30; Ernst von Weizsäcker, *Memoirs* (Chicago: Regnery, 1951), 208.
15. Göring's memory of the meeting, as told by him to his captors at Nuremberg. US Department of State, Special Interrogation Mission to Germany, 1945–1946, interrogation of Herman Göring, August 27, 1945, National Archives, 1104.
16. Dahlerus, *Last Attempt*, 88–94.
17. Dahlerus, 88–94.

13. "Where Is the Pole?"

1. Franz Halder, *The Halder War Diary, 1939–1942* (Novato, CA: Presidio, 1988), 42.
2. Birger Dahlerus, *The Last Attempt* (London: Hutchinson, 1947), 96–99.
3. Dahlerus, *Last Attempt*, 96–99; *Documents of British Foreign Policy* (*DBFP*), series 3 (London: Her Majesty's Stationery Office, 1954), 395–98. The best description of the calls to Göring are in a memo written by the British Foreign Office. See *DBFP*, 399–400.
4. Paul Schmidt, *Hitler's Interpreter* (New York: Macmillan, 1951), 153–54.
5. *DBFP*, 391.
6. Halder, *Halder War Diary*, 42, 44. Besides Göring's wire taps, the Germans were running two other intercepts of the Poles' communications.
7. Schmidt, *Hitler's Interpreter*, 150; Ernst von Weizsäcker, *Memoirs* (Chicago: Regnery, 1951), 208.
8. For the entire list of sixteen points, see *Documents of German Foreign Policy* (*DGFP*), series D, vol. 7 (Washington, DC: US Government Printing Office, 1949), 447–50.
9. Associated Press, *Richmond News Leader*, August 30, 1939.
10. *DGFP*, 442.
11. *Trial of the Major War Criminals before the International Military Tribunal* (*TMWC*), vol. 10 (Nuremburg, Germany: Secretariat of the Tribunal, 1947), 368.
12. *DGFP*, 446.
13. *TMWC*, vol. 12, 1055–56.
14. Halder, *Halder War Diary*, 40.
15. Great Britain Foreign Office, *The British War Blue Book* (New York: Farrar and Rinehart, 1939), 181–82.
16. Apparently, the document was transmitted in two "takes," one at 9:15 p.m. and the other at 12:40 a.m. the next morning. Great Britain Foreign Office, *The British War Blue Book*, 447.
17. Nevile Henderson, *Failure of a Mission: Berlin 1937–1939* (New York: Putnam, 1940), 283.
18. Joachim von Ribbentrop, *The Ribbentrop Memoirs* (London: Weidenfeld and Nicolson, 1954), 123.
19. Schmidt, *Hitler's Interpreter*, 150.
20. Schmidt, 150.
21. Schmidt, 151.
22. Schmidt, 150–53; Henderson, *Failure of a Mission*, 282–87; *DGFP*, 451–52; *DBFP*, 413–14, 432–33.
23. *DBFP*, 465–66.

24. William L. Shirer, *Berlin Diary: The Journal of a Foreign Correspondent, 1934–1941* (New York: Knopf, 1941), 191.
25. Henderson, *Failure of a Mission*, 287; DBFP, 433.
26. Dahlerus, *Last Attempt*, 100–103.
27. Great Britain Foreign Office, *The British War Blue Book*, 187–88.

14. The Intercepted Telegram

1. William Russell, *Berlin Embassy* (New York: Dutton, 1941), 11.
2. Ernst von Weizsäcker, *Memoirs* (Chicago: Regnery, 1951), 209.
3. Weizsäcker, *Memoirs*, 209.
4. Ulrich von Hassell, *The Ulrich von Hassell Diaries, 1938–1944: The Story of Forces against Hitler inside Germany* (Westport, CT: Greenwood, 2011), 44–45.
5. Von Hassell, *Ulrich von Hassell Diaries*, 44–45.
6. Birger Dahlerus, *The Last Attempt* (London: Hutchinson, 1947), 104–5.
7. Dahlerus, *Last Attempt*, 107. The Germans intercepted the telegram, and Göring gave Dahlerus his handwritten version of it. *The Polish White Book*, which was published after the start of the war—and like similar books defending the actions of the other governments—was aimed at justifying Warsaw's actions and omits the final instruction, but Lipski's actions later confirm that he was under such orders.
8. Göring at Nuremberg, *Trial of the Major War Criminals before the International Military Tribunal*, vol. 9 (Nuremburg, Germany: Secretariat of the Tribunal, 1947), 497–98.
9. Franz Halder, *The Halder War Diary, 1939–1942* (Novato, CA: Presidio, 1988), 43, 44.
10. Weizsäcker, *Memoirs*, 209.
11. Dahlerus, *Last Attempt*, 111–15; Nevile Henderson, *Failure of a Mission: Berlin 1937–1939* (New York: Putnam, 1940), 289.
12. *Documents of German Foreign Policy*, series D, vol. 7 (Washington, DC: US Government Printing Office, 1949), 477–78.
13. Paul Schmidt, *Hitler's Interpreter* (New York: Macmillan, 1951), 154.
14. Henderson, *Failure of a Mission*, 291.
15. Weizsäcker, *Memoirs*, 209.
16. Hans Bernd Gisevius, *To the Bitter End* (Boston: Houghton Mifflin, 1947), 374–75.
17. Galeazzo Ciano, *The Ciano Diaries, 1939–1943* (New York: Doubleday, 1946), 135.

15. Invasion

1. William L. Shirer, *Berlin Diary: The Journal of a Foreign Correspondent, 1934–1941* (New York: Knopf, 1941), 197.
2. Franz Halder, *The Halder War Diary, 1939–1942* (Novato, CA: Presidio, 1988), 44.
3. Army leaders expected the Luftwaffe to bomb Warsaw, but it did not. Apparently still trying to avoid any other action that would stir up the English, Göring had ordered his commanders to avoid civilian targets. Birger Dahlerus, *The Last Attempt* (London: Hutchinson, 1947), 116.
4. Great Britain Foreign Office, *The British War Blue Book* (New York: Farrar and Rinehart, 1939), 214–16.

5. Dahlerus, *Last Attempt*, 117; William Russell, *Berlin Embassy* (New York: Dutton, 1941), 47–49.

6. Office of Strategic Services memo, biographical sketches of Adolf Hitler and Heinrich Himmler, December 3, 1943, classified Secret, from Henry Field to Major John McDonough.

7. Office of Strategic Services memo; Shirer, *Berlin Diary*, 197–98.

8. Dahlerus, *Last Attempt*, 117–21.

9. *Documents of German Foreign Policy (DGFP)*, series D, vol. 7 (Washington, DC: US Government Printing Office, 1949), 485.

10. Galeazzo Ciano, *The Ciano Diaries, 1939–1943* (New York: Doubleday, 1946), 135–36; *DGFP*, 483.

11. Ciano, *Ciano Diaries*, 136.

12. Halder, *Halder War Diary*, 47.

13. Great Britain Foreign Office, *The British War Blue Book*, 206–7.

14. Paul Schmidt, *Hitler's Interpreter* (New York: Macmillan, 1951), 155.

15. Great Britain Foreign Office, *The British War Blue Book*, 217.

16. Schmidt, *Hitler's Interpreter*, 155.

17. Nevile Henderson, *Failure of a Mission: Berlin 1937–1939* (New York: Putnam, 1940), 293.

18. Henderson, *Failure of a Mission*, 293.

19. Dahlerus, *Last Attempt*, 122.

16. Ultimatum

1. Ernst von Weizsäcker, *Memoirs* (Chicago: Regnery, 1951), 210.

2. Galeazzo Ciano, *The Ciano Diaries, 1939–1943* (New York: Doubleday, 1946), 136–37; Paul Schmidt, *Hitler's Interpreter* (New York: Macmillan, 1951), 156.

3. Weizsäcker, *Memoirs*, 212.

4. Schmidt, *Hitler's Interpreter*, 157–58.

5. Schmidt, 158.

6. Heinrich Hoffmann, *Hitler Was My Friend* (Barnsley, UK: Frontline Books, 2011), 115.

7. Nevile Henderson, *Failure of a Mission: Berlin 1937–1939* (New York: Putnam, 1940), 297.

8. *Trial of the Major War Criminals before the International Military Tribunal*, vol. 16 (Nuremburg, Germany: Secretariat of the Tribunal, 1947), 69.

9. US Department of State, Special Interrogation Mission to Germany, 1945–1946, interrogation of Herman Göring, August 27, 1945, National Archives, 1114.

10. *Documents of British Foreign Policy*, series 3 (London: Her Majesty's Stationery Office, 1954), 429.

17. Finis

1. Interview with Captain John J. Masters, US Army, 1957.

2. Interview with confidential source, 2011.

3. Leonard Mosley, *The Reich Marshal: A Biography of Hermann Goering* (Garden City, NY: Doubleday, 1974), 357.

4. Decades later, a former guard named Herbert Lee Stivers told Bob Pool of the *Los Angeles Times* that he had done so. Two Germans had persuaded him to take a capsule to Göring, claiming he was sick and the prison had not been giving him his proper medication. *Los Angeles Times*, February 7, 2005, https://www.latimes.com/la-na-goering7feb07-story.html.

5. Ernst von Weizsäcker, *Memoirs* (Chicago: Regnery, 1951), 209.

BIBLIOGRAPHY

Axton, Matilda F., Rogers P. Churchill, Francis C. Prescott, John G. Reid, N. O. Sappington, Louis E. Gates, and Shirley L. Phillips, eds. *Foreign Relations of US Diplomatic Papers (USDP)*. Vol. 1. Washington, DC: US Government Printing Office, 1956.

Baur, Hans. *Hitler at My Side*. Houston: Eichler, 1986.

Below, Nicolaus von. *At Hitler's Side: The Memoirs of Hitler's Luftwaffe Adjutant, 1937–1945*. Mechanicsburg, PA: Stackpole Books, 1980.

Bloch, Michael. *Ribbentrop*. New York: Crown, 1992.

Bock, Fedor von. *The War Diary, 1939–1945*. Atglen, PA: Schiffer, 1996.

Ciano, Galeazzo. *The Ciano Diaries, 1939–1943*. New York: Doubleday, 1946.

Churchill, Winston S. *The Gathering Storm*. Boston: Houghton Mifflin, 1948.

Dahlerus, Birger. *The Last Attempt*. London: Hutchinson, 1947.

Dietrich, Otto. *The Hitler I Knew: The Memoirs of the Third Reich's Press Chief*. New York: Skyhorse, 2010.

Diplomatic Documents of Italy (DDI). Series 8, vol. 13.

Documents of British Foreign Policy (DBFP). Series 3. London: Her Majesty's Stationery Office, 1954.

Döhring, Herbert, Karl Krause, and Anna Plaim. *Living with Hitler: Accounts of Hitler's Household Staff*. Barnsley, UK: Greenhill Books, 2018.

The French Yellow Book. Diplomatic documents, 1938–39. London: Hutchinson, 1940.

Gilbert, G. M. *Nuremberg Diary*. New York: Farrar, Straus, 1947.

Gisevius, Hans Bernd. *To the Bitter End*. Boston: Houghton Mifflin, 1947.

Görlitz, Walter. *History of the German General Staff, 1657–1945*. New York: Praeger, 1953.

Great Britain Foreign Office. *The British War Blue Book*. New York: Farrar and Rinehart, 1939.

Halder, Franz. *The Halder War Diary, 1939–1942*. Novato, CA: Presidio, 1988.

Hanfstaengl, Ernst. *Hitler: The Missing Years*. London: Eyre and Spottiswoode, 1957.

Hassell, Ulrich von. *The Ulrich von Hassell Diaries, 1938–1944: The Story of Forces against Hitler inside Germany*.

Henderson, Nevile. *Failure of a Mission: Berlin 1937–1939*. New York: Putnam, 1940.

Hershman, D. Jablow, and Julian Lieb. *A Brotherhood of Tyrants: Manic Depression and Absolute Power*. Amherst, MA: Prometheus Books, 1994.

Hoffmann, Heinrich. *Hitler Was My Friend*. Barnsley, UK: Frontline Books, 2011.

Keitel, Wilhelm. *The Memoirs of Field Marshal Keitel*. New York: Stein and Day, 1966.

Krueger, Kurt. *I Was Hitler's Doctor*. New York: Biltmore, 1943.

Kubizek, August. *Young Hitler: The Story of Our Friendship*. Maidstone, UK: Mann, 1973.

Lehrer, Steven. *The Reich Chancellery and Führerbunker Complex: An Illustrated History of the Seat of the Nazi Regime*. Jefferson, NC: McFarland, 2006.

Manstein, Erich von. *Lost Victories*. Novato, CA: Presidio, 1982.

Messenger, Charles. *The Last Prussian: A Biography of Field Marshal Gerd von Rundstedt, 1875–1953*. London: Brassey's, 1991.

Mosley, Leonard. *On Borrowed Time: How World War II Began*. New York: Random House, 1969.

———. *The Reich Marshal: A Biography of Hermann Goering*. Garden City, NY: Doubleday, 1974.

Office of Strategic Services memo (OSS memo). Biographical sketches of Adolf Hitler and Heinrich Himmler, December 3, 1943, classified Secret, from Henry Field to Major John McDonough.

Office of United States Chief of Counsel for Prosecution of Axis Criminality. *Nazi Conspiracy and Aggression (NCA)* ("The Red Series"), supplement B. Washington, DC: US Government Printing Office, 1948.

The Polish White Book: Official Documents concerning Polish-German and Polish-Soviet Relations 1933–1939. London: Hutchinson, 1940.

Pool, Bob. "Former GI Claims Role in Goering's Death." *Los Angeles Times*, February 7, 2005. https://www.latimes.com/la-na-goering7feb07-story.html.

Ribbentrop, Joachim von. *The Ribbentrop Memoirs*. London: Weidenfeld and Nicolson, 1954.

Rittich, Werner. *New German Architecture*. Berlin: Terramare Office, 1941.

Russell, William. *Berlin Embassy*. New York: Dutton, 1941.

Schmidt, Paul. *Hitler's Interpreter*. New York: Macmillan, 1951.

Schwarz, Paul. *This Man Ribbentrop, His Life and Times*. New York: Messner, 1943.

Shirer, William L. *Berlin Diary: The Journal of a Foreign Correspondent, 1934–1941*. New York: Knopf, 1941.

———. *The Rise and Fall of the Third Reich: A History of Nazi Germany*. New York: Simon and Schuster, 1960.

Speer, Albert. *Inside the Third Reich*. New York: Macmillan, 1970.

———. *Spandau: The Secret Diaries*. New York: Macmillan, 1976.

Taylor, A. J. P. *The Origins of the Second World War*. New York: Atheneum, 1962.

———. *The Struggle for Mastery in Europe, 1848–1918*. Oxford: Clarendon Press, 1954.

Trial of the Major War Criminals before the International Military Tribunal (TMWC) ("The Blue Series"). 42 vols. Nuremburg, Germany: Secretariat of the Tribunal, 1947–1949.

US Department of State. *Documents of German Foreign Policy (DGFP)*. Series D, vol. 5, June 1937–March 1939. Records of Relations with Poland; the Balkans; Latin America; the Smaller Powers. Washington, DC: US Government Printing Office, 1949.

US Department of State. *Documents of German Foreign Policy (DGFP)*. Series D, vol. 7, August 9–September 3, 1939. The Last Days of Peace. Washington, DC: US Government Printing Office, 1949.

US Department of State. Special Interrogation Mission to Germany, 1945–1946. Interrogation of Herman Göring. National Archives.

US War Department. *Handbook on German Military Forces*. Washington, DC: US Government Publishing Office, 1945.

Warlimont, Walter. *Inside Hitler's Headquarters, 1939–45*. New York: Praeger, 1964.

Weitz, John. *Hitler's Diplomat: The Life and Times of Joachim von Ribbentrop*. New York: Ticknor and Fields, 1992.

Weizsäcker, Ernst von. *Memoirs*. Chicago: Regnery, 1951.

INDEX

RUSH LOVING JR. is a former reporter and business editor of the *Richmond Times-Dispatch* and was an associate editor of *Fortune* magazine. He served in the Carter White House as an assistant director of the Office of Management and Budget. In recent years, Loving has authored numerous magazine articles and two books, *The Men Who Loved Trains* and *The Well-Dressed Hobo*, both published by Indiana University Press.